Mobile Phenomena

by Temporary Services

with contributions by

Courtney Dailey

Alexis Petroff

Joseph Roberstson

Jen Hofer

Eric Steen

Christian Ettinger

Platform

Liberate Tate

The Center For Tactical Magic

Nils Norman

Half Letter Press, LLC

Mobile Phenomena by Temporary Services

Copyright © 2012 by Temporary Services and Half Letter Press, LLC

Some rights reserved. You are free to share, to copy, distribute, display, and perform the work, under the following conditions:

- Attribution. You must attribute this work to Temporary Services and the contributors, and include the full title of the book, publisher, and year of publication.
- Noncommercial. You may not use this work for commercial purposes.
- No Derivative Works. You may not alter, transform, or build upon this work.
- For any reuse or distribution, you must make clear to others the license terms of this work.
- Any of these conditions can be waived if you get permission from the copyright holder.

Printed and bound in the United States of America
Published by Half Letter Press

Half Letter Press, LLC
P.O. Box 12588
Chicago, IL, 60612
USA

www.halfletterpress.com
publishers@halfletterpress.com

ISBN-13: 978-0-9818023-2-9
ISBN-10: 0-9818023-2-X

Edited and designed by Temporary Services

Temporary Services
P.O. Box 121012
Chicago, IL, 60612
USA

www.temporaryservices.org
servers@temporaryservices.org

Temporary Services is Brett Bloom, Salem Collo-Julin and Marc Fischer. We are based in Chicago, Copenhagen, and Philadelphia. We have existed since 1998. We produce exhibitions, events, projects, and publications. Previous books by Temporary Services include: *Public Phenomena* (Half Letter Press, 2008), *Group Work* (Printed Matter, 2007), and, in collaboration with the artist Angelo, *Prisoners' Inventions* (WhiteWalls, 2003). In this book, and in all other areas of life, the distinction between art practice and other creative human endeavors is irrelevant to us.

Temporary Services seeks to create and participate in ethical relationships that are not competitive and are mutually beneficial. We develop strategies for harnessing the ideas and energies of people who may have never participated in an art project before, or who may feel excluded from the art community. We mobilize the generosity of many people to produce projects on a scale that none of us could achieve in isolation. We strive towards aesthetic experiences built upon trust and unlimited experimentation.

Temporary Services thanks the following people and organizations for their help and support for this publication and our research over the years for this book: Michael Rakowitz, Jeanne Dunning, Northwestern University, The Block Museum of Art, Deborah Stratman, Jen Hofer, Steve Badgett, Rob Ray, Jesse Bercowetz, Nance Klehm, and Brennan McGaffey.

Additional copyediting support provided by Jen Blair and Bonnie Fortune.

Photographs are credited to their authors on the pages where they appear. Those photographs not accompanied by credit information in the body of the book were taken by Temporary Services except for the bottom image on page 7, which is courtesy of the Intermod Series (www.intermodseries-org), and the bottom image on page 8, which is courtesy of IC-98 (www.socialtoolbox.com).

Front cover: *Mobile Phenomena: Bike Truck*, by Temporary Services, 2006
Back cover: *Tactical Ice Cream Unit*, by The Center for Tactical Magic

---

Temporary Services: Pick-Laudati Artists in Residence of the Alice Kaplan Institute for the Humanities at Northwestern University, 2009.

CONTENTS

6   And Now We Take Our Leave:
         An introduction by Temporary Services

11   Binder Archives

15   Bookmobiles

18   Mobilivre-Bookmobile:
         Courtney Dailey interviewed by Temporary Services

26   Mobile Phenomena

46   Bar Bike:
         Christian Ettinger interviewed by Eric Steen

53   Mobile Protest

64   Mobility Resources

AND NOW WE TAKE OUR LEAVE
An Introduction by Temporary Services

What does it take to create a useful environment of social mobility that is not based in top-down or bottom-up ideas of class structure? Is it possible to bypass both? Can we find fluid ways to move across strata?

These may seem to be very strange questions in the context of a publication called *Mobile Phenomena*. Mobile phenomena are ideas and services that function in a portable way. They may be pushed on wheels, towed by a bike or car, or simply carried in your arms or on your back.

When we think about mobile structures and mobility in general, the concept of "social mobility" comes to mind. Social mobility is most often defined as the gradual movement of individuals and groups in society from a place of less access (to wealth, opportunity, or well-being) to one of greater access. Our definition of social mobility includes sideways and lateral movements. Sometimes it is desirable and/or necessary to shift back to a place of less access or less consumption. Sometimes the same shift needs to be made in a physical or emotional landscape, but not necessarily within the commonly defined limits of class or social structure.

If we seek to remake the world we currently live in to suit our individual and collective needs, does that require breaking apart or dismantling social structures? Can social mobility be achieved through rebuilding physical structures to suit our needs? Can one float through and around class structure and refuse to land?

The projects and phenomena we have chosen to highlight in this publication call these questions to our attention. People remake the world around them to suit their needs. In two earlier publications by Temporary Services (called *Public Phenomena*), we examined self-made public gestures such as roadside memorials, makeshift barriers, and parking place savers.

Mobile phenomena create movement for their inventors and users in both a literal and a figurative sense. We create infrastructure where there is none, like food trucks, clinics on wheels, and bookmobiles. We use these tools to move through emotional and social landscapes with greater ease.

We inherit city spaces that we have had no role in shaping. Long ago, decisions were made about how things are situated and used in these spaces. There are certainly huge benefits to this – like paved roads and garbage collection – but there are additional limits that shape and structure the ways in which we can act and behave. There are structured limits in how we are allowed to contest the preconceived uses of space (prohibitive zoning, codes, or de facto segregation) and open up new uses. Mobile phenomena can unhinge the expected roles we take in shared city spaces. They can become a new norm when they work.

Our own interest in mobile projects grew out of our long-running

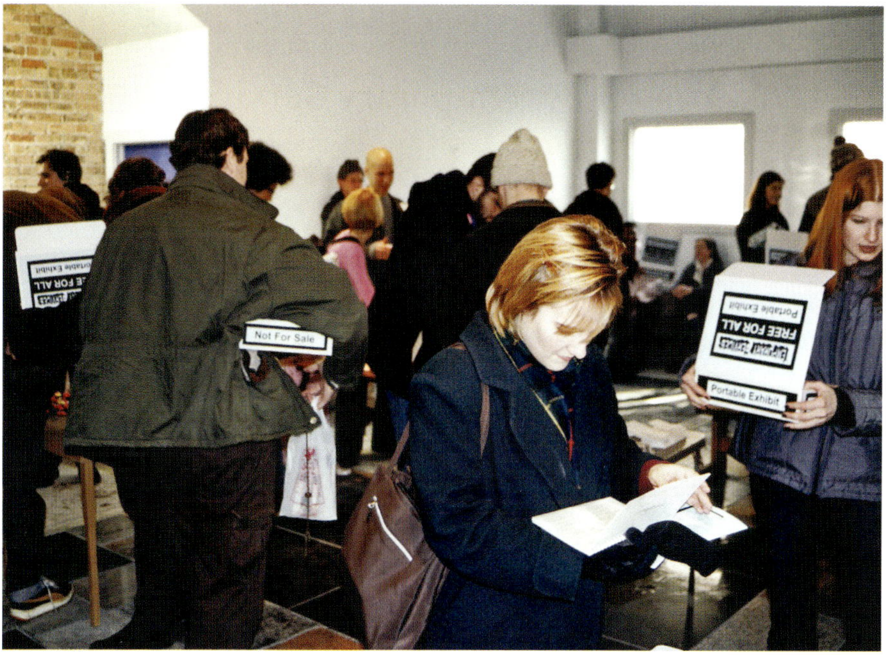

Free For All: Visitors at this one day event got free silkscreened boxes when they entered the storefront and filled them with objects of their choosing, produced in quantity by over fifty artists, individuals and organizations. Over 10,000 items were given away. February 5, 2000.

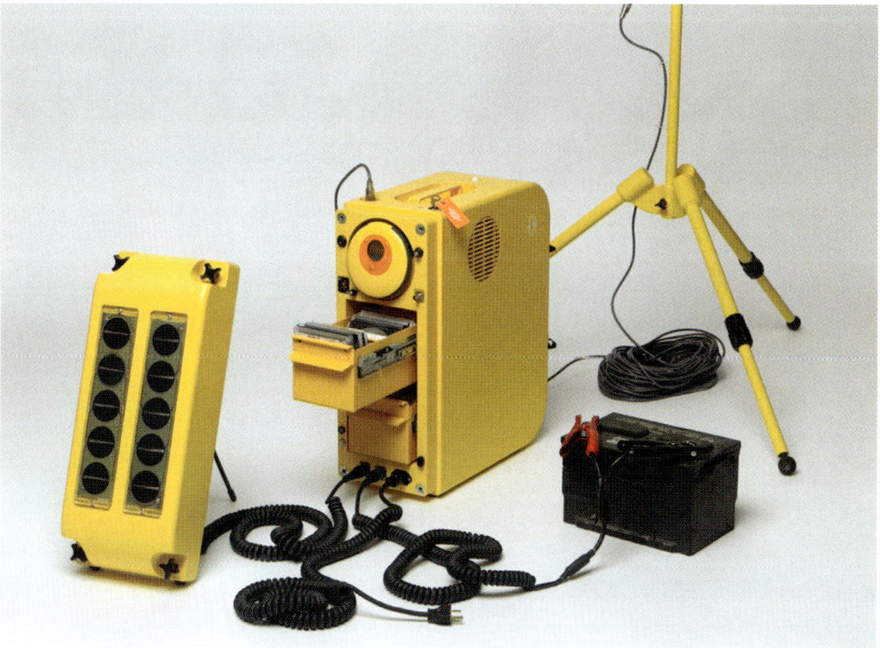

Audio Relay: The *Audio Relay* is designed to be as small and lightweight as possible for maximum portability. It stores several hundred unique CDs playable on the built-in CD player, and has a 4-watt transmitter for FM broadcasting. Developed by Intermod Series, 2002-ongoing.

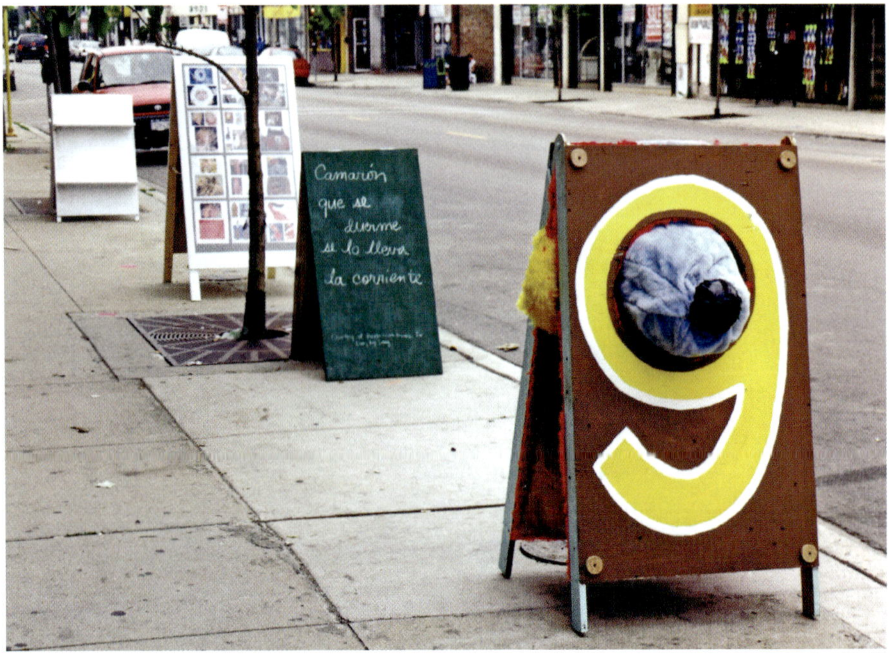

Mobile Sign Systems: sandwich board signs lined up in front of the old Temporary Services storefront space along North Milwaukee Ave. in Chicago by artists (left to right): Oli Watt, Matti Allison and Marc Fischer, Jacqueline Terrassa, and Rob Kelly and Zena Sakowski. June 1999.

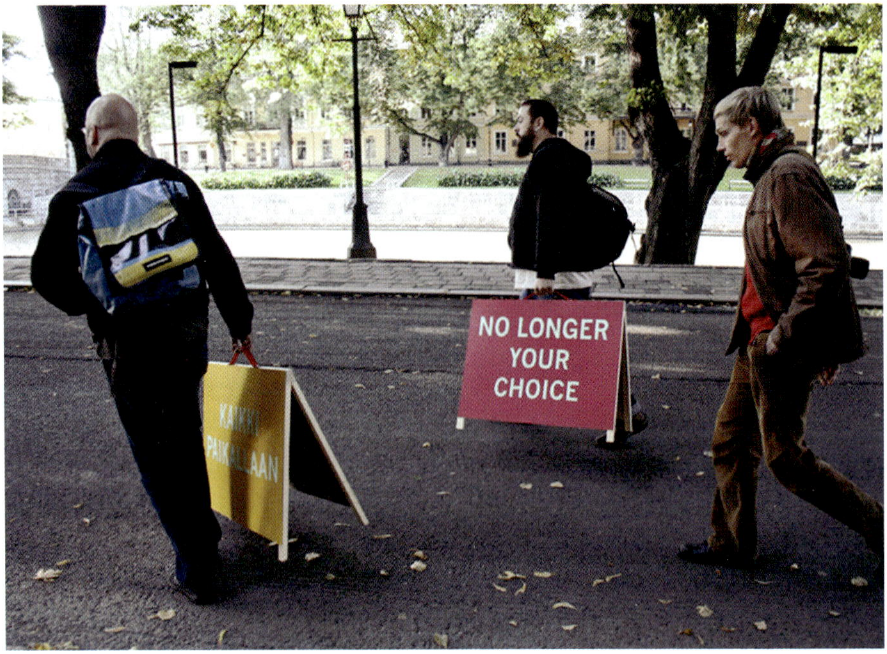

It Is Always Like This: Marc and Brett (from Temporary Services, left and center) carrying sandwich board signs for placement in Turku, Finland with Visa from IC-98 (right). The lightweight signs had nylon straps that encouraged people to pick them up and use them. 2008.

concern with developing ways of expanding the audience for art and experimental creative practices beyond galleries and museums. Early in our work together, we became dissatisfied with depending solely on indoor exhibition spaces, and took our work to the streets and other host sites, using wheeled projects like *Binder Archives*, sandwich board signs designed by many artists in a project titled *Mobile Sign Systems* (1999), and an exhibition that could be carried away in a box titled *Free For All* (2000).

In 2001 we had conversations about portability, the airwaves as public space, and autonomy with artist Brennan McGaffey, who works under the name Intermod Series. Out of that dialog, McGaffey designed and fabricated a portable radio transmitter and audio archive titled the *Audio Relay* that Temporary Services situates and programs.

A 2004 collaboration with JAM (Jane Palmer and Marianne Fairbanks) entitled *Dragged City* used bicycles that towed suitcases on roller blade wheels – each outfitted with a different mobile function including a library, bar, first aid station, and mini music collection with sound system.

In 2008 we revisited the sandwich board sign format for a collaboration with the Finnish group IC-98 (Patrik Söderlund and Visa Suonpää) titled *It Is Always Like This*. Working together, we made twenty-four light wooden signs with phrases that advertise nothing and weren't always terribly positive. Many of the texts, written collaboratively by the two groups, pointed to our frustration with the monotony of city spaces and the high degree of political control that is exerted over them. The signs originated in front of Titanik Galleria in Turku but were quickly picked up by passersby and placed around the city to varying effect and for a range of lifespans.

In 1999 and 2000, we began compiling web addresses and other listings for mobile projects and created a Mobile Structures Resources page on temporaryservices.org in collaboration with Jesse Bercowetz – an artist who shared our interest in mobile creativity across disciplines. Many of the links are now dead, but the pages are still active and remain useful for thinking about the breadth of mobile projects that exist around the world. In addition to categories we explore in this book, the pages include: medical services, disaster relief, services for the homeless, military applications, animal-oriented services, religious organizations, fitness and recreation units, telescopes on wheels, mobile document shredding services, petting zoos, art projects, and of course mobile homes.

In this book you will find a selection of photos of mobile phenomena documented by ourselves, as well as by friends and collaborators. This selection is obviously nowhere near comprehensive, and we hope that you'll consult some of the printed and online resources suggested in the back of this book for more documentation by other authors. Our book is an addition to the material on the subject – a selection of photos drawn from years of observing these things during travels made for other purposes and while working on different projects. These include bookmobiles,

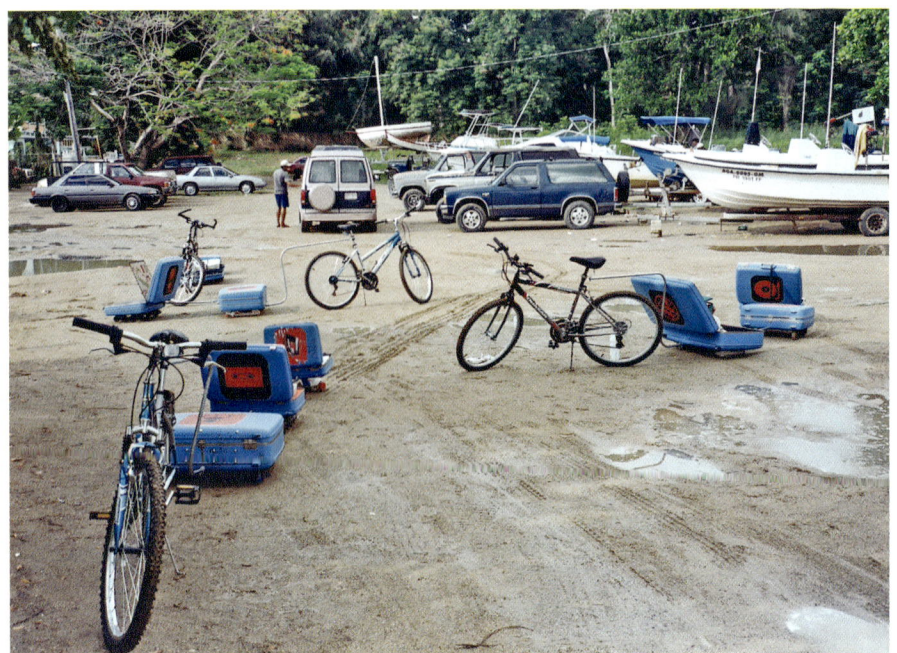

Dragged City: Collaboration between Temporary Services and JAM for PR 04 in San Juan and Rincon, Puerto Rico. Four bikes were used to pull eleven units, each with a different function, fabricated from reused suitcases, roller blade wheels, and metal conduit connectors. 2004.

mobile forms of commerce, inventive mobile structures that take the form of art projects, mobile structures created for use during protest, and some strange applications of mobility that defy easy description, categorization, or whose function could not be readily discerned.

Many things were seen quickly in passing, and we were not always able to ask more questions of the mobile practitioner at the time of the encounter. We do, however, include windows into a few practices: the extraordinary *Mobillivre-Bookmobile*, The Center For Tactical Magic's *Tactical Ice Cream Unit*, and an interview conducted by our beer-loving correspondent Eric Steen who spoke with Christian Ettinger in Portland about Hopworks Urban Brewery's bar bike.

There has been an explosion of interest in making mobile projects over the past few years. Given the dismal state of the economy in the U.S. and abroad, it should come as no surprise that people are creating restaurants in trucks, setting up libraries attached to bikes, and myriad other approaches to everyday cultural and political work that is freed from brick and mortar structures and leases. For the cost of one month in a storefront, people can build a small mobile structure and use it for years. It is our hope that this book can be an inspiration to other citizens, artists, activists, nomads, and anyone who is interested in escaping the constraints of their location, culture, the economics of property, or other factors that make realizing one's desires difficult.

BINDER ARCHIVES

Binder Archives was a portable exhibition on wheels that Temporary Services created, curated, and utilized from 2002-2006. The text that follows is reprinted from the *Binder Archives Project Manual* – a self-published booklet that we first printed in 2002. This booklet, and an exhibition guide with information on all of the participants, was given away at each showing of *Binder Archives*.

The project was relatively easy to maintain. The binders sometimes needed to be repaired or replaced after heavy usage or rough travel, but this was inexpensive. Of greater impact, however, were changes to airline policies regarding baggage size and weight. On one of the project's final travels, for an exhibition entitled *Public Services* in Radkersburg, Austria, the project was determined to be both oversized and overweight. We scrambled at the airport to lower the weight by transferring some of the binders to our carry-on luggage, but the dimensions of the box could not be changed and we were forced to pay a hefty additional fee. It was clear from this point on that long-distance presentations of *Binder Archives* would be subject to the same expensive shipping fees that normal exhibitions must contend with. Of course *Binder Archives* still fits perfectly well in the backseat of a car.

Binder Archives worked in ways we had expected. However, viewers always gave the binders more attention at comfortable indoor installations (whether in an exhibition space, a spare room at a library, or just someone's apartment living room) than in outdoor presentations. In outdoor spaces, the reasons why the project was on dispaly confounded people as nothing was for sale, nor were we marketing or campaigning for any particular cause. Nonetheless, it was a lot of fun to activate shared city spaces with this unusual collection of material – something that has been achieved on a much larger scale more recently with the many guerrilla outdoor public libraries that have erupted from the Occupy movement and Occupy Wall Street in New York City in particular.

From the *Binder Archives Project Manual*:

Binder Archives is a portable exhibition that is designed to travel with the greatest of ease. In *Binder Archives*, three-ring binders and their European equivalents are used as a mode of presenting or containing large quantities of material and information. For this project, individual artists, exhibition organizers, creative people, archivists, and groups are producing binders that they will fill with photographs, drawings, documentation, photocopies, printed ephemera, tactile objects, or any other material that can be punched with three holes or stored in clear plastic sleeves. Each binder is a self-contained project or archive of a person's or group's work. Some of these individual binders contain as much material as one might expect to

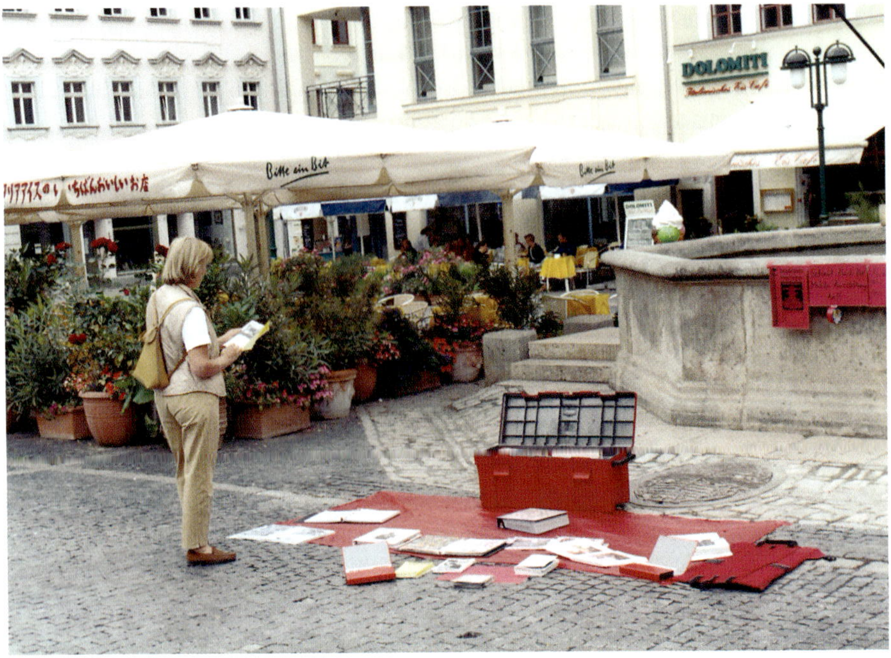

Binder Archives In Weimar, Germany: In 2003, curator Frank Motz brought Temporary Services to Weimar and Leipzig, Germany for the exhibition *Get Rid of Yourself*. The show was split between two venues: the Alternative Cultural Center in Weimar and Halle 14 in Leipzig.

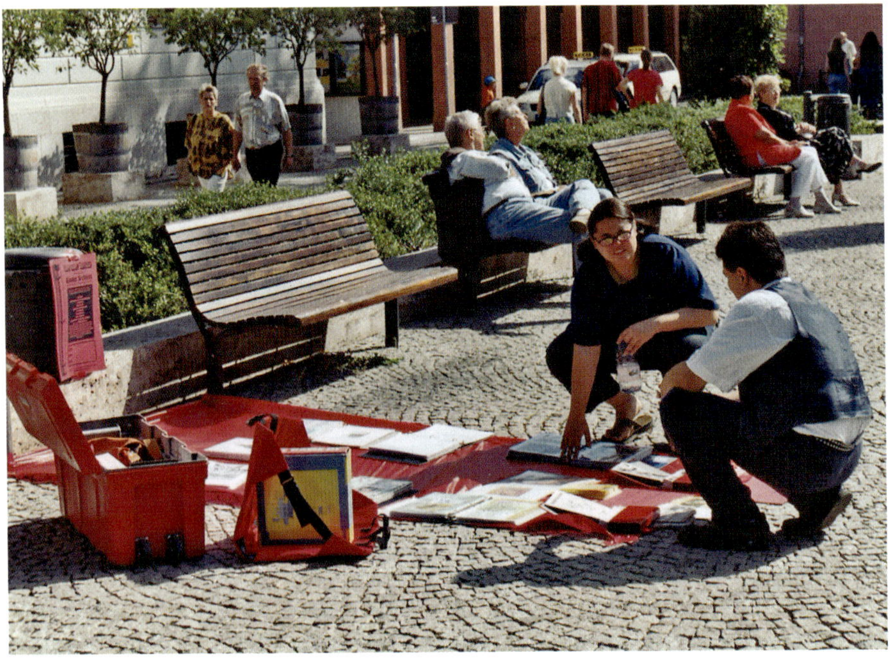

While in Weimar, we made guerrilla presentations of *Binder Archives* at a number of city spaces including a park, a café, and a couple public squares. Here is one showing with Salem Collo-Julin from Temporary Services (left) presenting the project to a man who was passing by.

find in an entire exhibit or a book. Viewers can freely handle the binders just as they might browse through books in a reference library.

Binders are easily available from any office supply store. They are inexpensive, sturdy, and available in many different sizes. Their design is very basic and has not changed significantly over the years. Binders make it possible to create your own hardbound book without the expense or finality of publishing. Pages can be removed and rearranged until a satisfying presentation is determined. The contents of the binders can be photocopied and made into new binders. If a binder gets worn out from excessive use, it can be replaced easily; its contents can be transferred into the new binder.

The project *Binder Archives* is easily unpacked and installed in a matter of minutes. Everything that is needed for the exhibit fits in a single, modified, hard, foam plastic case. The case is large enough to hold between ten and twelve binders containing over one thousand pages of material. It can also store over 100 free booklets, posters, and one or two camping chairs. The case is suitable for indoor or outdoor use. It is lightweight, resistant to rust and corrosion, and made from plastic with a strength that is topped only by metal. The case can be checked into the body of an airplane as luggage. The case weighs approximately sixty pounds when it is filled. One person can wheel *Binder Archives* down the street and unpack as much or as little of the work as can be displayed at a particular site. A site with tables or desks is ideal, but a floor will suffice. Walls are unnecessary. As with all Temporary Services projects, a free booklet about *Binder Archives* will accompany all presentations. A poster will be used to mark locations or advertise publicly. A separate exhibition guide has been produced. This guide can be changed and re-published as old binders get replaced with new ones.

The participants in *Binder Archives* can play a critical role in determining where the entire project is shown. Since a fixed location is not required for any considerable length of time, the people that are a part of *Binder Archives* can use their contacts, friends, and collaborators to extend the exhibition of these works beyond our own means. They can help to secure new locations for short term presentations.

With *Binder Archives*, Temporary Services has developed a new strategy for bringing large and complete projects to different audiences in an active manner. This means finding new spaces that are available inexpensively or for free, using other institutions on a short-term basis, using the homes of friends in other cities, using publicly trafficked space in new ways and finding affordable ways to present exhibitions internationally.

Binder Archives Participants: Jesse Bercowetz and Matt Bua, Lori Couve, Jim Duignan & The Stockyard Institute, Céline Duval, Marc Fischer, Melinda Fries, Harold Jefferies, Rob Kelly & Zena Sakowski, Jakob Kolding, Alexis Petroff, Peter F.A.N. Redgrave, Bruno Richard, Elyce Semenec,

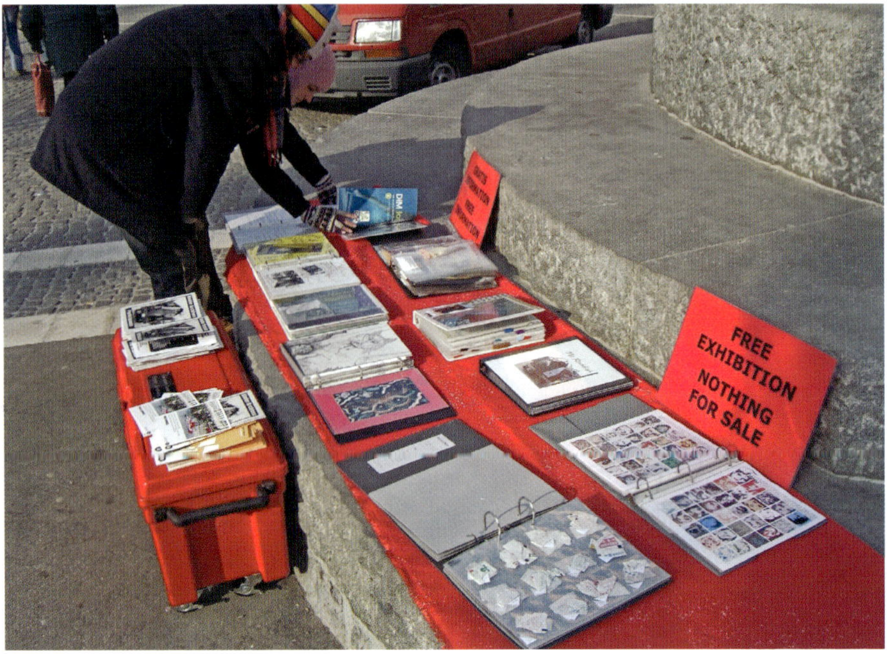

Binder Archives In Slovenia: In 2006, *Binder Archives* traveled with the exhibition *Public Services*, curated by Tadej Pogacar and Polonca Lovšin. One stop was P74 Center and Gallery in Ljubljana, Slovenia. This photo is from a public showing there coordinated by Lovšin.

Street Flyer & Public Notice Archive, and WE LIKE DICK – a project by Erika Mikkalo that includes: ANAIS, Angela Altenhofen, Jennifer Bauer & Karen Gollrad, Julie Cabell, Raina Cowan, [name removed by request], Diane Green, Shawna Holman, Antonia B. Johnston, Maire Kennedy, K. Madeleine Kohler, Lo Art, KellyMarie Martin, Erika Mikkalo, Phloe, Cynthia Plaster Caster, Melissa Schubeck, Sister Serpents, Anne Vander Linden, Laural Winter, and Elizabeth Yokas.

For more information and images visit: www.temporaryservices.org/b_a_contributors.html

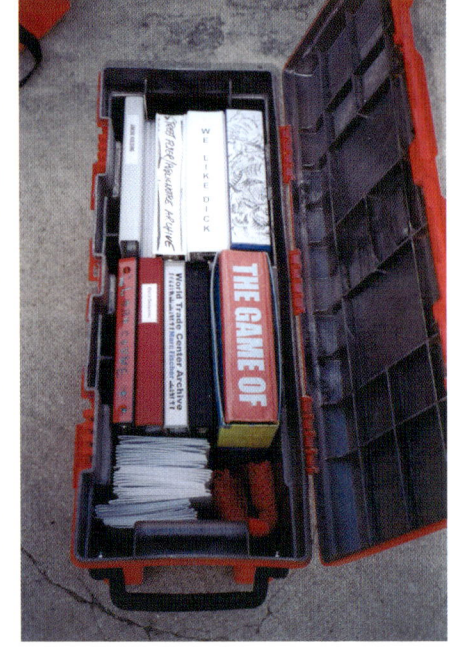

Ready To Go: The *Binder Archives* case packed up and prepared to be transported from one site or city to another.

BOOKMOBILES

In the United States, bookmobiles, usually connected to branch libraries, express an ideal of building an informed public to strengthen democracy. Where libraries were not yet built, bookmobiles could take publications to remote populations so they could be as educated as those in larger towns and cities. Mobile libraries also provide access to knowledge for the elderly and people with mobility challenges. In her book *Bookmobiles and Bookmobile Service* (see Resources list), Eleanor Frances Brown writes:

> Bringing books and people together by means of a bookmobile is the most dramatic of all commonly-used types of library service. It is also very efficient in relation to cost. Although bookmobiles cannot provide services equal to those provided by modern branch libraries, when properly used they are an indispensable adjunct of branch service. Bookmobiles are found traveling over lonely, sometimes almost impassable, country back roads and over the smooth pavements of busy city streets. In some areas, when they have served their purpose, they will disappear from the scene. But they will spring up again in areas of greater need.

What follows is a small selection of historic bookmobiles. There are myriad contemporary models and we highlighted one, *Mobilivre-Bookmobile*, that operated without a brick and mortar home base.

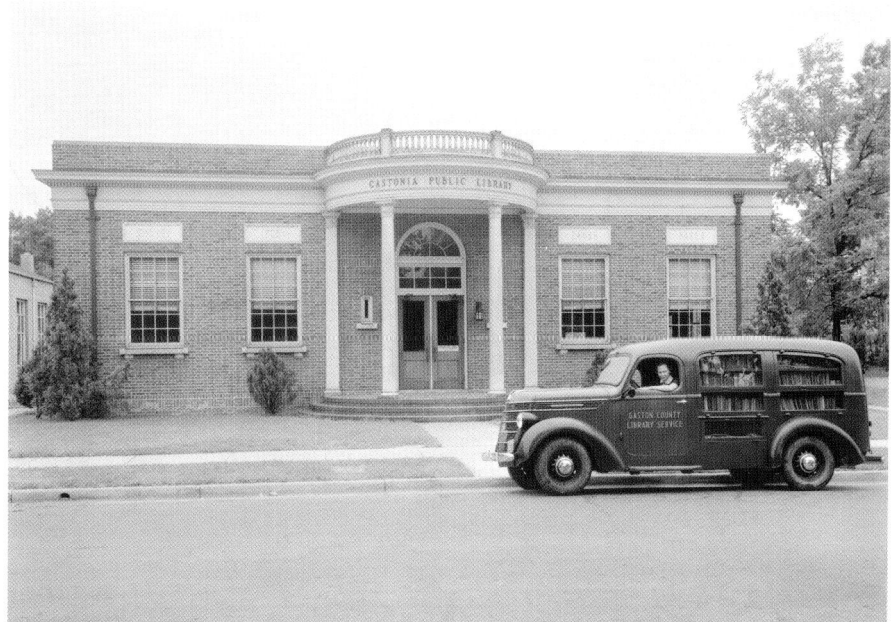

Take The Library To The People: Gaston County Bookmobile, Gastonia, Gaston County, North Carolina, Library of Congress Prints and Photographs Division Washington, D.C., Carnegie Survey of the Architecture of the South collection. Photo by Benjamin Johnston, 1935.

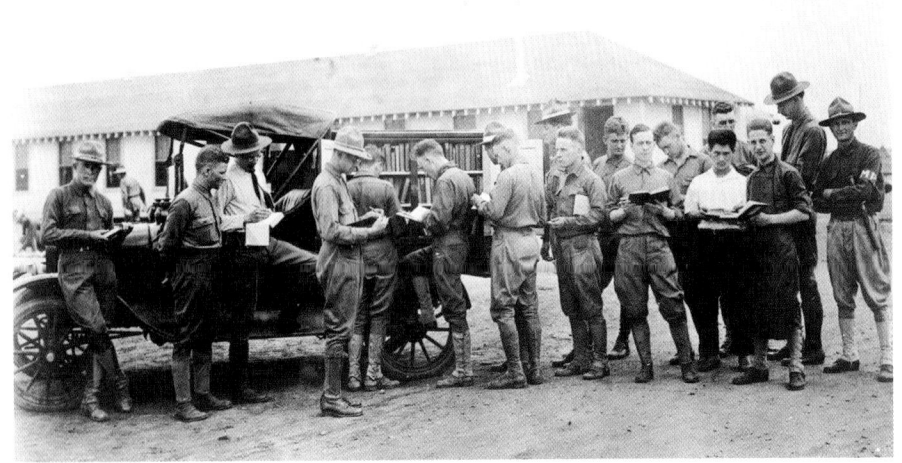

U.S. Soldiers Getting Library Books From Truck: Kelly Field Library, Library of Congress Prints and Photographs Division Washington, D.C. Photographer unknown, taken between 1909 and 1920.

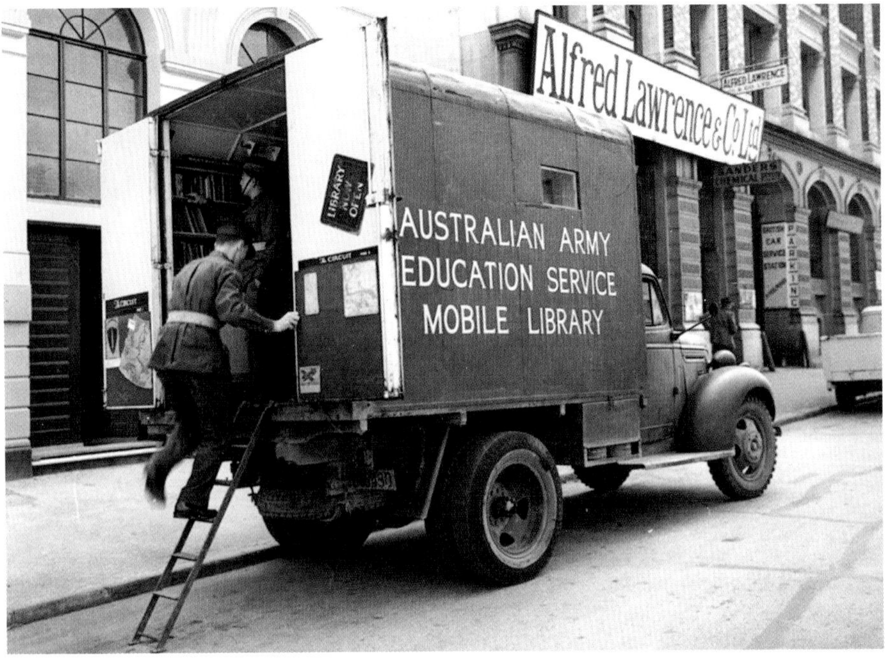

Australian Army Educational Mobile Library: Soldier accessing the library using steps at the back of the truck while another soldier is inside browsing the shelves. Signs on the open doors advertise the circuit the library takes around town. Brisbane, Australia, 1942.

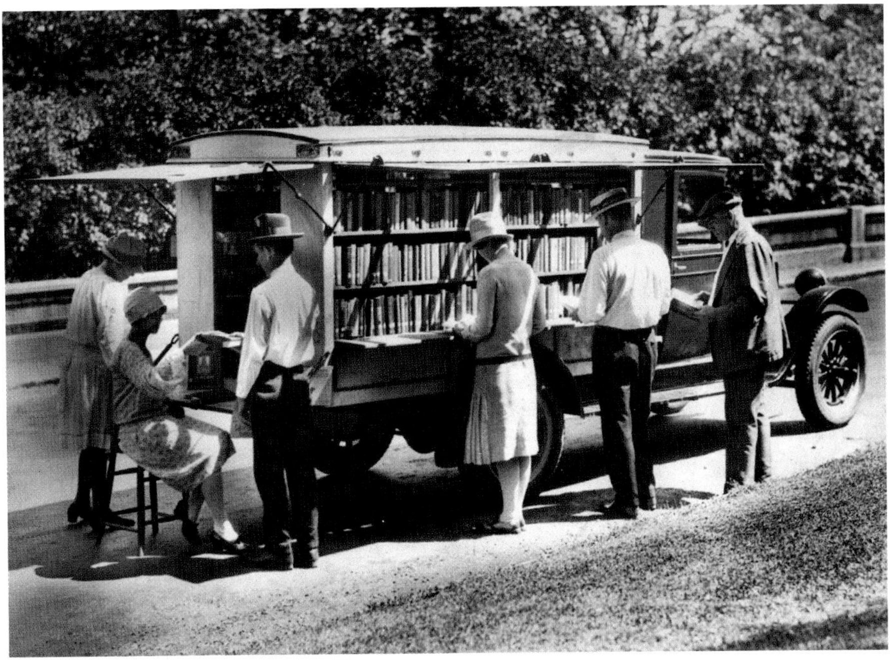

The Librarian Is In Even When The Library Is Out: The first bookmobile of the Public Library of Cincinnati & Hamilton County began its service to rural schools in 1927 and eventually expanded it to other areas. Image courtesy of the Ohio Historical Society.

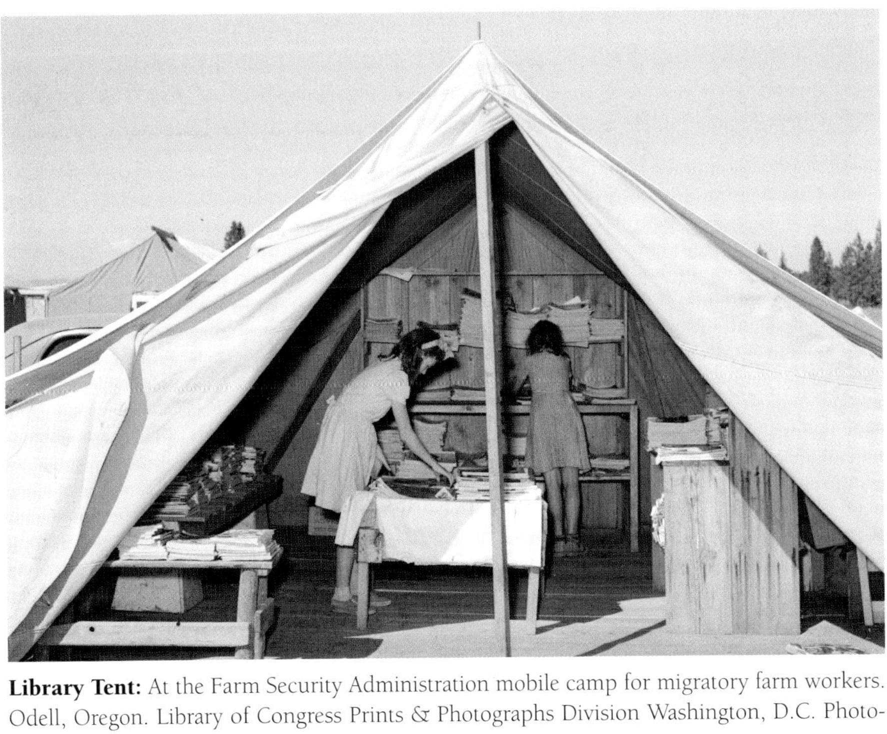

Library Tent: At the Farm Security Administration mobile camp for migratory farm workers. Odell, Oregon. Library of Congress Prints & Photographs Division Washington, D.C. Photograph by Russell Lee, 1941.

MOBILIVRE-BOOKMOBILE
Courtney Dailey interviewed by Temporary Services

One of the great challenges of working with larger mobile creative projects is keeping them on the road. Mobile projects require a lot of caretaking, involve constant audience engagement, need updating to stay vital, are sometimes hard to store when not in use, and can be expensive to maintain. *Mobilivre-Bookmobile* is one of the rare art-related mobile projects that rose to all of these challenges and succeeded in touring dozens of cities and sharing the work of thousands of artists and authors for a period of over five years.

We cannot remember how we learned about the *Mobilivre-Bookmobile* (MB) project but can definitely recall the first time we experienced it. The MB visited Chicago in September during one of its early tours in 2001. Participants from the *Mobilivre-Bookmobile* were conducting a bookbinding workshop inside Quimby's Books, a much-loved vendor of all that is independently produced and self-published. The trailer was parked near Quimby's and finding a spot on the street for this vehicle in the bustling Wicker Park neighborhood was no easy task.

On the archival website mobilivre.org, the project is described as follows:

> The *projet MOBILIVRE-BOOKMOBILE project* explores the long held tradition of bookmobiles as traveling libraries that promote the distribution of information. The BOOKMOBILE travels across the United States and Canada in a vintage airstream trailer visiting a variety of communities. Our annual traveling collection of approximately 300 book works range from handmade and one-of-a-kind to photocopied and small press publications.

A member of Temporary Services met the friendly people who were touring with the project inside Quimby's and talked with them about their work. With flashlights in hand, we went out to explore the airstream. The playful and carefully considered interior design by the group Freecell was as exciting as the rich and diverse curated selection of books and 'zines. Elastic bands held the publications into place on stepped shelves so that they wouldn't go flying while the project was on the road. One could easily spend hours perusing everything on view – something we had more time to do a couple years later when the MB passed through Chicago again.

More than just a trailer with a bunch of books, the MB was also a collective. The website describes its crew as:

> [A] diverse group of emerging North American artists and community

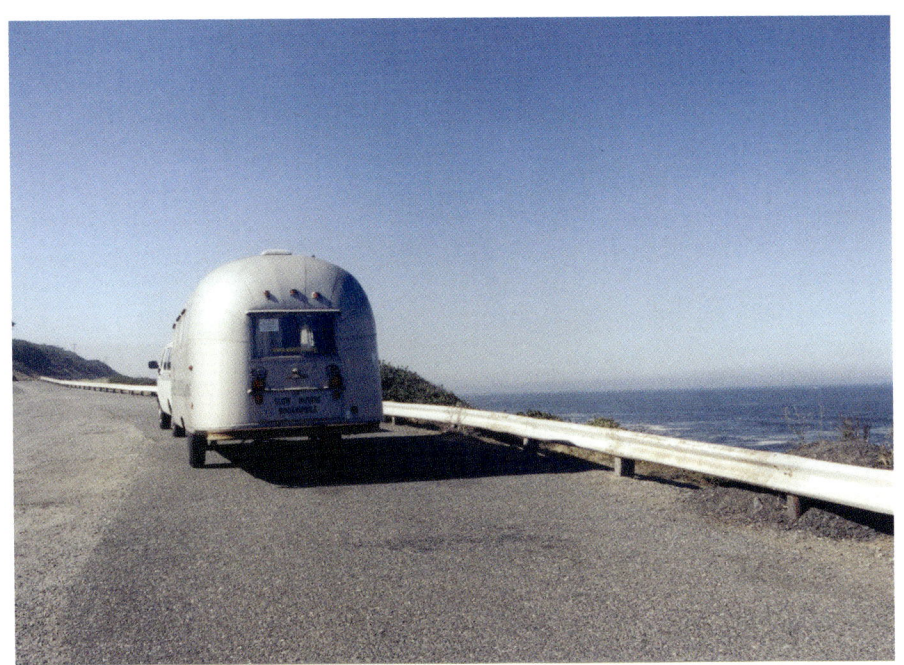

activists. Our mandate is to fuse artistic production with political activism and community organizing. The collective consists of a fluctuating group of dedicated volunteers, coordinators, jury organizers, and tour guides. Although the project is based primarily in Montreal, QC, and Philadelphia, PA, collective members reside in various cities throughout North America.

Courtney Dailey was one of the MB people we met early on. We've stayed in touch over the last decade and were happy to connect over email to ask for her recollections of the project and how it all worked over so many years and miles. Courtney answered our questions in July, 2011. The photo of the bookmobile interior is by Adam Wallacavage. The shots of presentations and the exterior are courtesy of the collective. All photos are from between 2001 and 2003.

Temporary Services (TS): How did you choose what books would be displayed in the Bookmobile?

Courtney Dailey (CD): A jury was chosen by members of the Bookmobile collective and was composed of writers, illustrators/graphic novelists, librarians, readers, artists, and independent publishers (I am sure that I am leaving someone out here). The jury varied each year, and the selection process alternated between being in Montreal and Philadelphia.

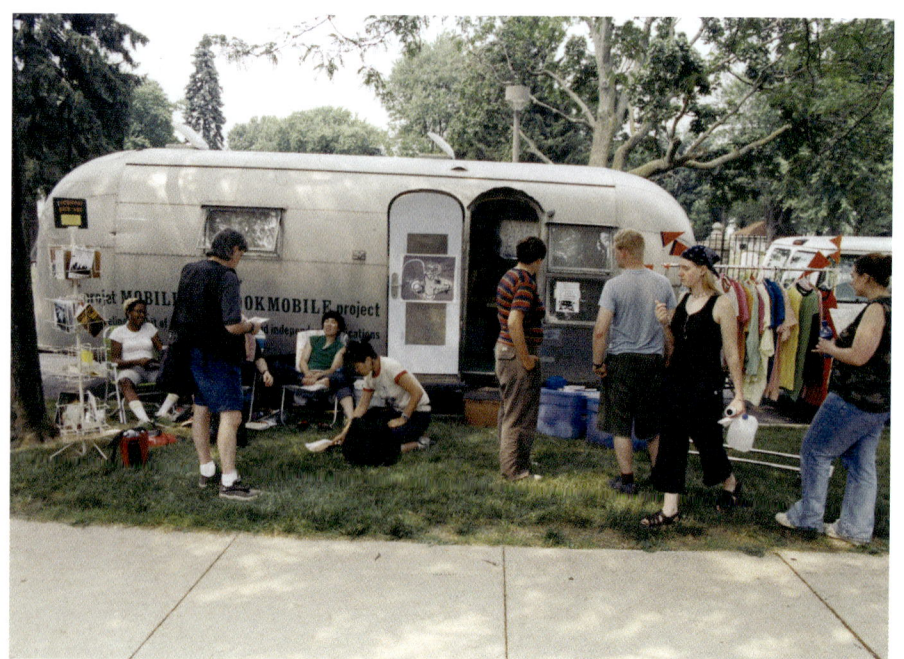

TS: How many works were presented at any given time and how often did you change the selection?

CD: There were around 300 books and zines presented each year, and the collection changed annually. We did have a "regional rack" of books and zines that folks would donate while we were on the road, which happened because visitors were excited and wanted to give us their books when we met them in their town! We decided to have a rotating display that was housed outside of the trailer (a metal comic-book shop fixture that easily dis-assembled) to share their donations. The juried collection was inside of the trailer, and those books were, mostly, on loan for the year. At the end of the tour, books were returned to their authors/makers, unless they agreed to donate them to our archive.

TS: Bookmobile collective members toured with the project as it moved throughout the country and into Canada. How did that network of volunteers function? Was it easy to find people to travel with the project?

CD: The touring volunteers were called "tour guides" and included collective members and friends, or friends-of-friends; as far as I can remember, we never took complete strangers on tour with us. There was usually a collective member on tour (at least one) along with two other tour guides. It was pretty easy to find folks to go on tour – isn't the dream of all visual artists to be like a band and get to go and visit towns full of enthusiastic supporters?! Truthfully, we were lucky to know a lot of people who had flexible enough schedules that would allow them to get away for two to six (or maybe even eight) weeks at a time, to travel and teach people about books, zines, and how to make both of them, themselves.

TS: To what degree did activities and presentations of the books take place inside the trailer and how much did you use outdoor space, or indoor hosts as the trailer moved from city to city? Did people sleep in the trailer too?

CD: The juried books and zines always remained in the trailer, and we had stools and benches for people to sit on while they read/looked. It was pragmatic on a few fronts: one, we could keep an eye on these precious items that people had really generously loaned us for a while, reminding people to be careful and tidy with the books (which most people definitely were); two, we could be in a more "controlled" environment where theft was harder for those who might feel like they just had to have the last four issues of *Paper Rodeo*; and three, we were able to host visitors in bad weather. The installation of the trailer was also important to us: we had custom-made upholstery and curtains (by early collective member Rebecca Watt), and an incredible interior design by Freecell, a design-build architecture firm who remain great friends. It was cozy and welcoming (we hoped, and learned from visitors), which was a priority for us, materially as well as conceptually. If we were going to try to break down the precious and meticulous world of book-arts, and the punker-than-you world of zine culture, we needed to show people that they were welcome to hang out with these objects and investigate them.

TS: How much did the project utilize institutional hosts like art spaces or stores, and to what degree did it function autonomously or with other forms of support like donations of space, money, or other resources from volunteers or visitors?

CD: We visited a variety of venues, from the National Gallery of Canada to Quimby's bookstore in Chicago, to a Riot Grrrl festival at a park in San Diego. We always had support from local hosts, which could manifest as people telling their friends that we were coming, folks letting us crash on their floors, putting up posters, playing music at a party during the visit, feeding us, telling us where the most excellent swimming holes were, on to financial contributions and support so that we could keep filling up the gas tank. The volunteer labor that makes a project like the *Bookmobile* happen is unreal, and way too impossible to quantify, both on the level of collective members through tour guides, tour hosts, and supporters of all stripes. No one was ever paid for doing this project, though while on tour everyone received a per diem of $20, to do whatever they wanted to do with … which usually ended up being food.

TS: How was the project funded?

CD: Since we were a bi-national project, we had some tough times in the world of grants; additionally, we seemed to be "too arty" for social justice funders and "too social justice-y" for the art funders, so they were never a great source of income. We did begin to receive some small grants from the Canada Council, which was great. Most funding came from our actual tour, either from sponsoring institutions or from people who visited and threw a $5 or a $20 into our plastic piggy banks. We were never a non-profit, but did hold fundraising art auctions and parties fairly regularly, which enabled us to get some chunks of cash together. We learned a lot about how different funding is in Canada and the U.S.!

TS: Gas must have been a huge expense. What are some tips you could offer for surviving on the road with a project like this?

CD: Make everything as simple as you can make it, and rely on the kindness of people you meet. It is truly humbling to feel the generosity of enthusiastic folks as you travel around. Try to figure out a way to be self-funding and not rely on grants or loans. And, in the end, it never hurts to have another job that can help you pay your rent!

TS: Was it hard to find a place to park the trailer for extended periods of time?

CD: Yes! There are laws that we learned all about by having a trailer in Philadelphia and Montreal…It always has to be attached to a vehicle if it's on a city street. Parking, luckily, was usually pretty easy, and I had some incredibly watchful neighbors who would tell us if folks were skulking around! The trailer got written on with graffiti a few times, but that was really the extent of the damage.

TS: Any problems getting busted for sleeping in the trailer?

CD: I think that there were some tense times, particularly in New York City, but for the most part it was pretty easy and we were left alone. We never slept in the trailer, as that was full of the books, but we had a bed in the back of our 15-passenger van, with curtains on the windows, so we were pretty well hidden.

TS: What kinds of audiences did the project reach?

CD: The audiences were somewhat varied, and generally included: interested art crowds, interested pedagogical/educational folks (including students whose classes were visiting), passersby, book-enthusiasts and

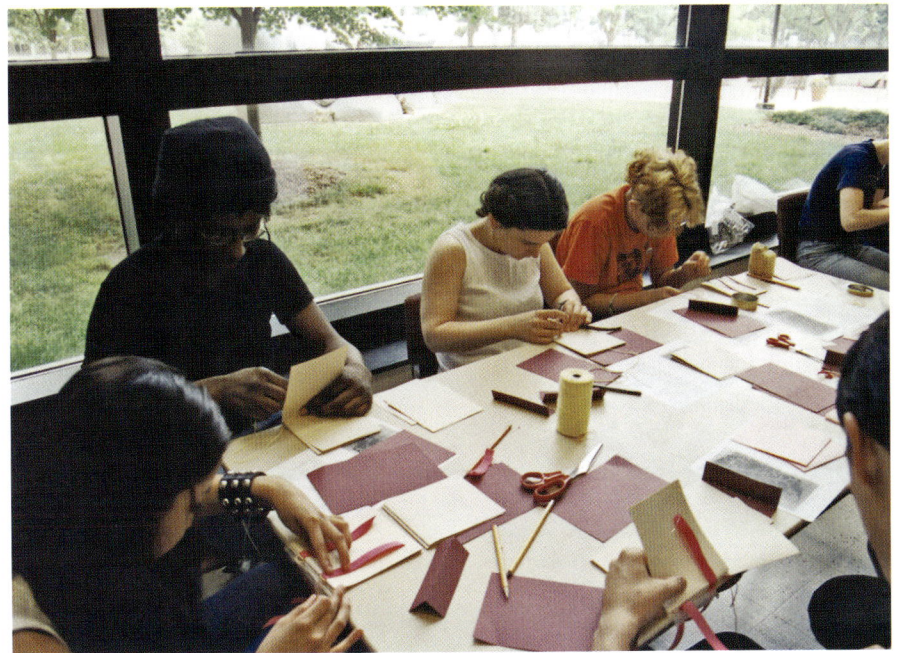

readers, zine fiends, Indymedia types. The audiences were as diverse as our venues were, which was important to how we booked our tours. The majority of the books were in English, though we did have more French books toward the end of the project, as we had made that a particular goal of the group. Our venues were primarily English-speaking, but we did one fairly extensive tour in Quebec and New Brunswick that had more Francophone stops.

TS: Any favorite stories about how people responded? I remember at one presentation in Chicago some people that stumbled upon the trailer were very confused that the books in the Bookmobile were not for sale. Was this a regular obstacle for viewers?

CD: There are so many stories ... many people were just surprised that it was free, that you could just look at the books and/or that you could learn how to bind books at a workshop that we were giving, for free. People definitely wanted to buy them, all the time. Usually when we explained that it was an exhibition, and that they could contact the artist directly through the contact info in a binder that was in our coffee table, they were excited about the idea ... usually.

TS: Were some locations or audiences hostile to the project or to the kind of material you were showing?

CD: We definitely had to do some sweeps of the collection when we were

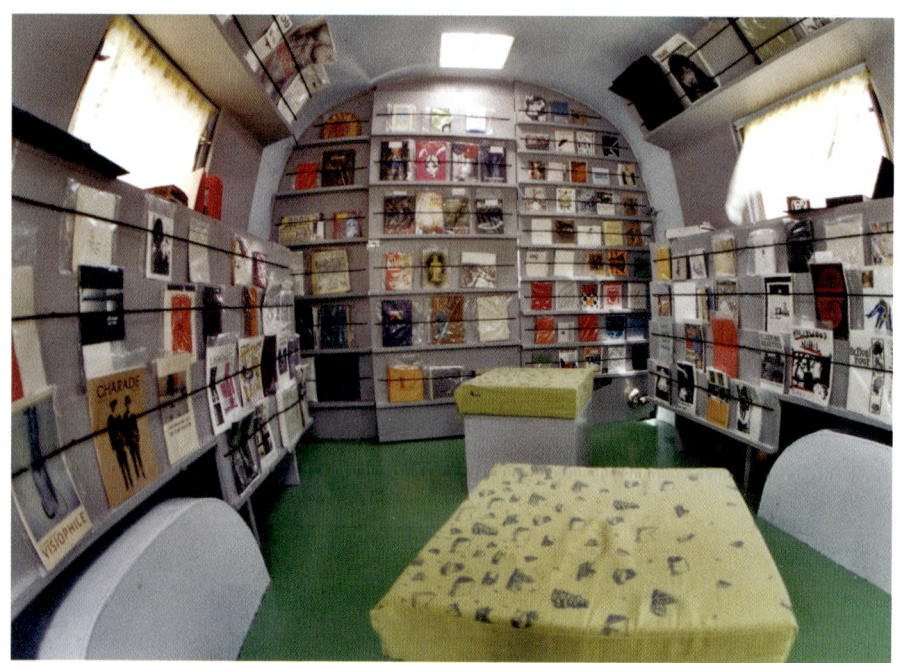

visiting elementary schools or church groups; those selections were our own choice to make, in my recollection, though there may have been requests from a few hosts. We removed sexually-explicit materials, mostly because the kids would get so wrapped up in the imagery that there was no moving away from it for their entire visit to the trailer. I am sure that there were experiences that viewers had, disagreeing with something in the books or zines, but most people can navigate those issues by putting down the book and looking at a different one. We had a lot of conversations with visitors about things that the books/zines brought up: anti-colonialism/imperialism, Israeli apartheid, sexual health, prison abolition, etc. I don't remember too many of them being combative or disruptive, but there were probably some like that.

TS: What were some of the inspiring experiences from being on the road with the Bookmobile?

CD: These will be shared in our upcoming book about the project—they are really best catalogued by the Tour Guides, who spent hours and hours interacting with the visitors and passers-by to the *Bookmobile*. To be honest, we got to meet some of the most amazing people in some unlikely places ... I'll never forget rolling into York, Alabama, where we were invited to Easter brunch with: an incredible letterpress printer and artist, Amos Kennedy; a family who was working with Amos to produce their daughter's high school graduation invitation; a Scrabble champion; an environmental activist who had spent time in jail for organizing against a nuclear power plant in her town; and the administrative assistant to a US Senator who introduced the bill for funding the first ever bookmobiles in the country. This is a tiny, tiny town that still does all of the street cleaning by hand, mind you, and a place that we would never have encountered if we hadn't met Amos at a stop that we did at the Rural Studio, in nearby Newburn, Alabama. It was the shortest stop that we ever made on tour, about 4 hours, but it was inspiring to see an incredible group of people who had created such a vibrant and resource-rich place.

TS: Now that the project has ended, what did you learn from it? What are some of the lessons that you carry with you from being part of the project?

CD: Oh god, this is such a giant question! We learned SO MUCH from this project that I don't think that I can enumerate all … but one thing that I realized is that when we thought we were doing something to "share skills" and "promote access to making things," we were really trying to teach ourselves. A pedagogical project, in my estimation, is always about teaching yourself and maybe only slightly about teaching others. I also learned everything I know about organizing giant, way-too-ambitious projects with a group of people who are geographically dispersed but who share a love in their hearts for collaboration … and these are skills that I continue to use, daily.

TS: What is the current status of the Airstream?

CD: The Airstream is sitting on a piece of land outside of Toronto, as a part of a project by the Black Fly collective, an anarchist building project that is teaching people to build straw-bale houses. We sold it to them in 2008, right as I was moving from Philadelphia to San Francisco for school. It seemed right to pass it along to another crew who would take care of it, and use it for something good.

TS: What advice would you give to others who are thinking of working with mobile projects?

CD: Do it! Be fearless! If you are interested in something, chances are high that others will be too … keep building, and be open to what might emerge from the meetings you have … on the move, the encounters you facilitate will be rich!
 AND, don't hit the road without: a handy how-to-fix-your-car manual, boomin' stereo system (it always helped us feel more secure, even as the vans were breaking down, to have a strong bass carry us through), and a spot to sleep. Our home away from home was the back of the van, which allowed a semblance of familiarity when gone from our loved ones and loved towns.

MOBILE PHENOMENA

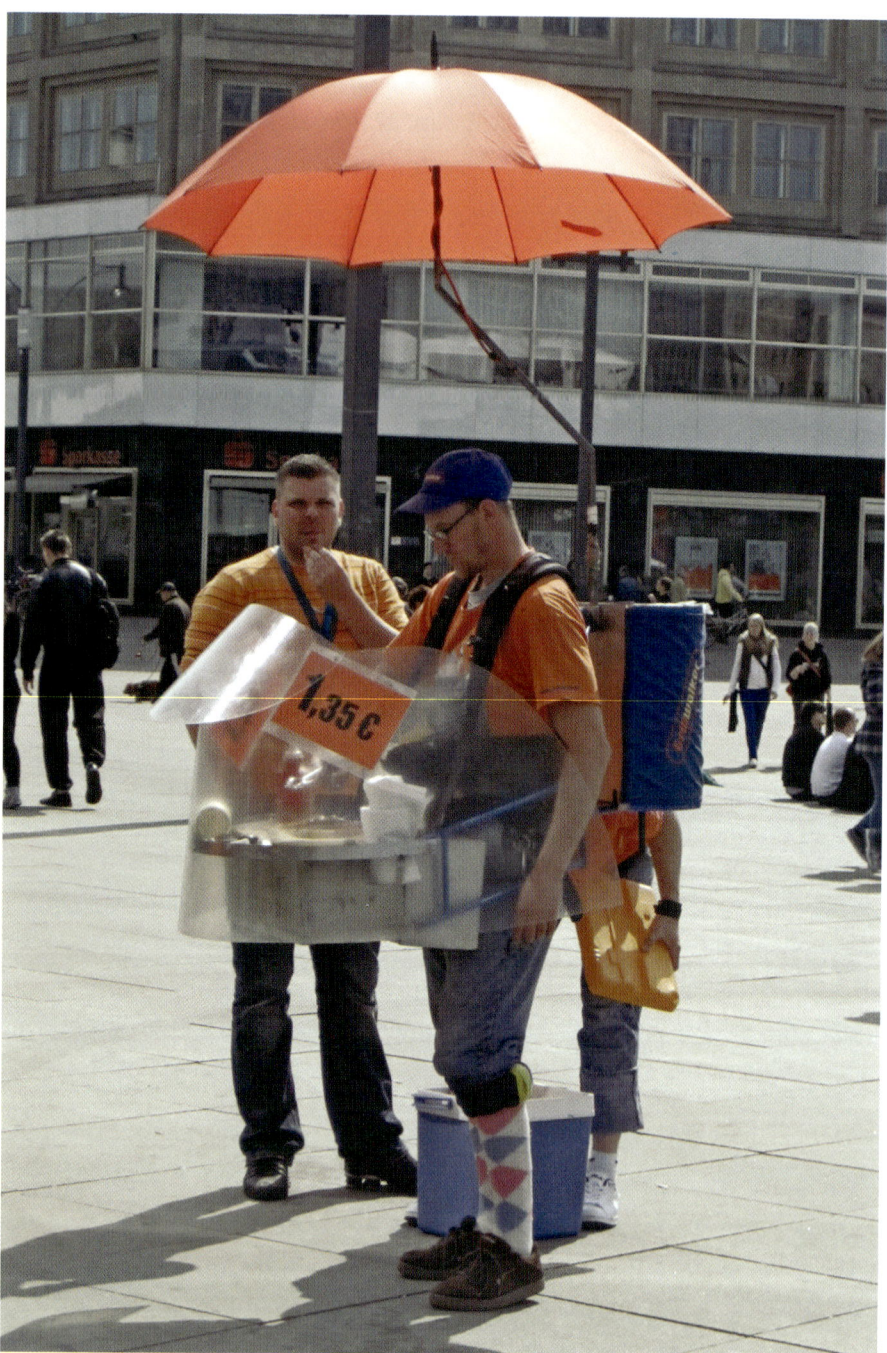

Wearable Grill: Personal, wearable grills are a common site in Berlin's Alexanderplatz. You can find them throughout the city. They are extremely lightweight and portable and can go into spaces larger hot dog vendor vehicles cannot. Berlin, May 2012.

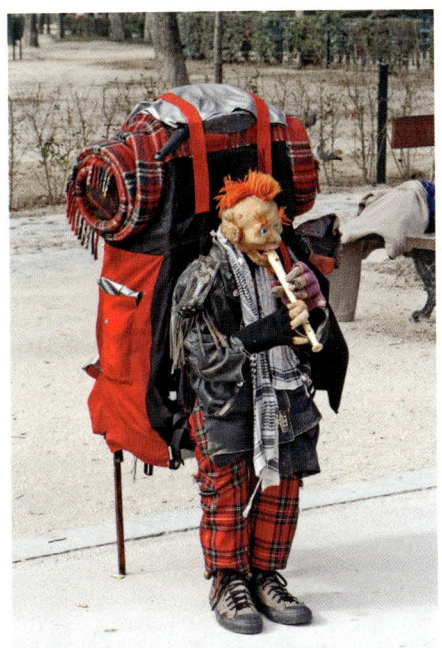
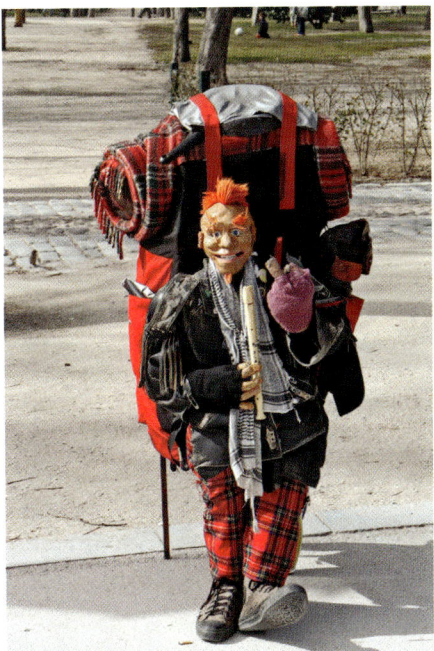

Punk On The Go: This street performer, who appears to go by the name "Punki" was spotted doing his delightfully crude act in Retiro Park in Madrid, Spain. The performer's upper body is neatly concealed inside a backpack. Punki plays a recorder, juggles, gives passersby the middle finger, and hurls various insults. Occasionally he also leaps up suddenly from his chair support and goes running toward the audience. These photos were taken by Temporary Services in February 2006.

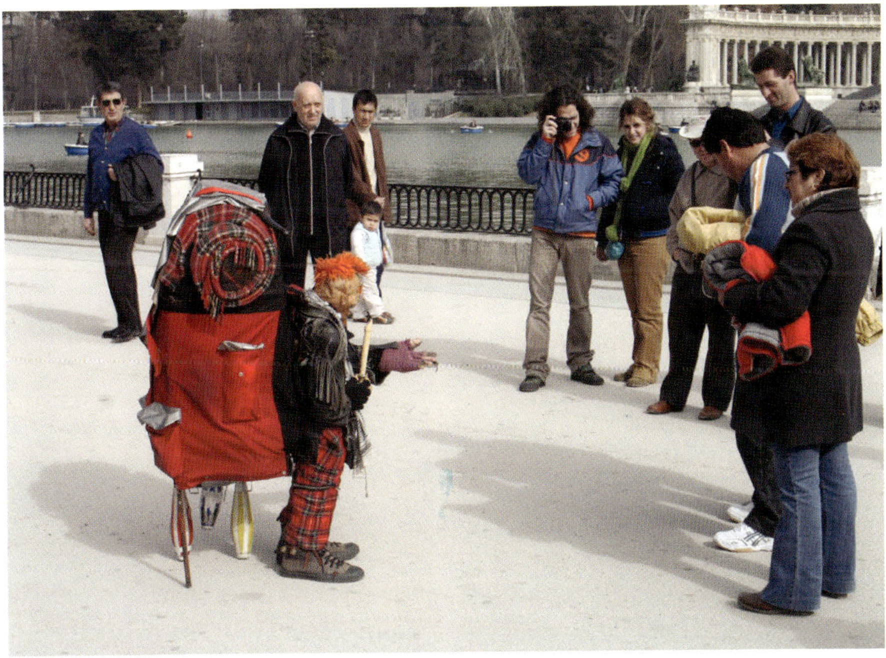

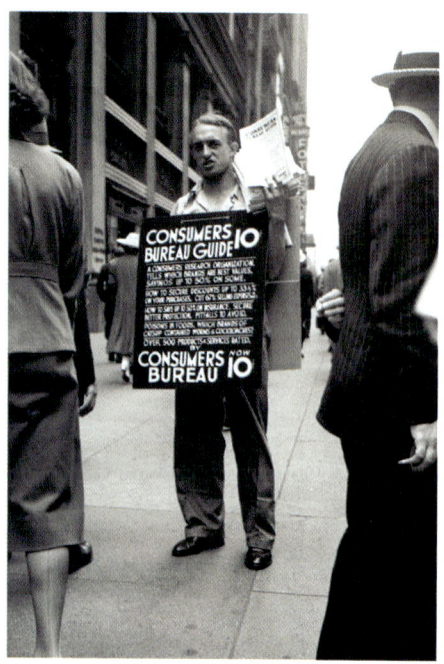 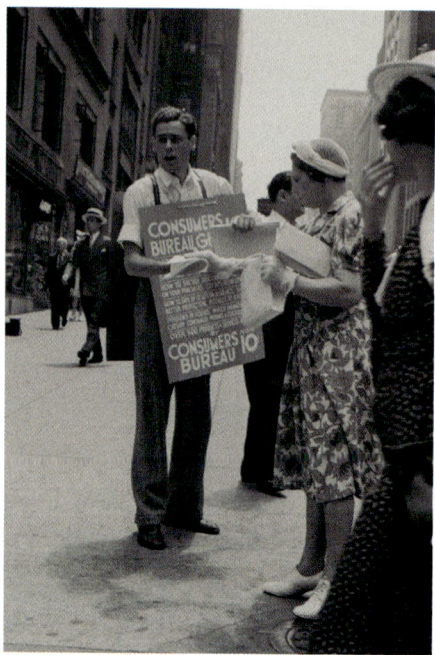

Mad Men With Sandwich Boards: 42nd Street and Madison Avenue. Street hawkers selling Consumer's Bureau Guide. New York City. Library of Congress Prints and Photographs Division Washington, D.C. Both photographs are by Dorothea Lange, 1939.

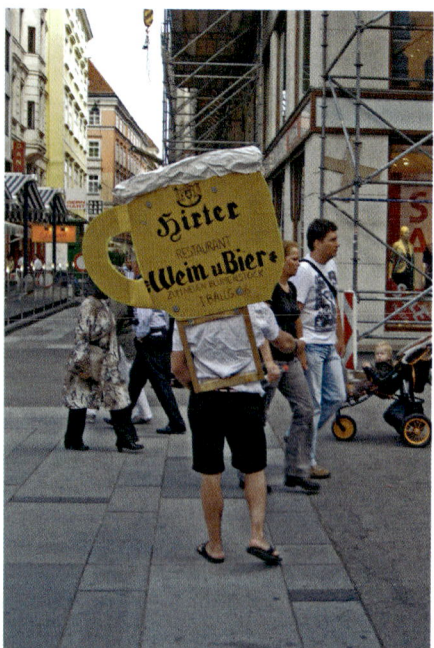 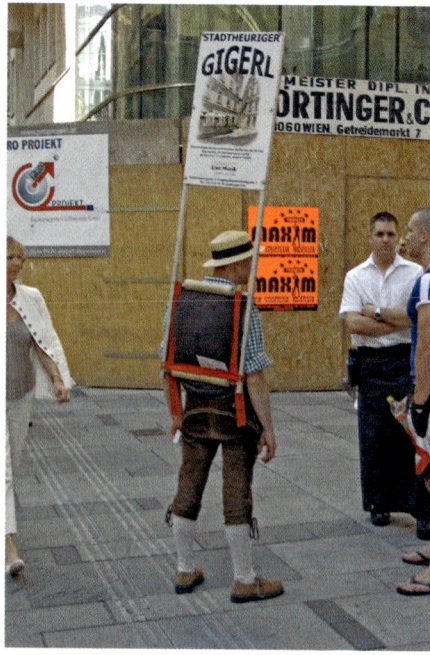

Sandwich Board Beer Men: Backpack signs are used in a busy shopping corridor in Vienna, Austria, to pitch bars and restaurants. More proactive than a stationary sign, mobile admen accost pedestrians, and display menus in an effort to attract customers. June 2010.

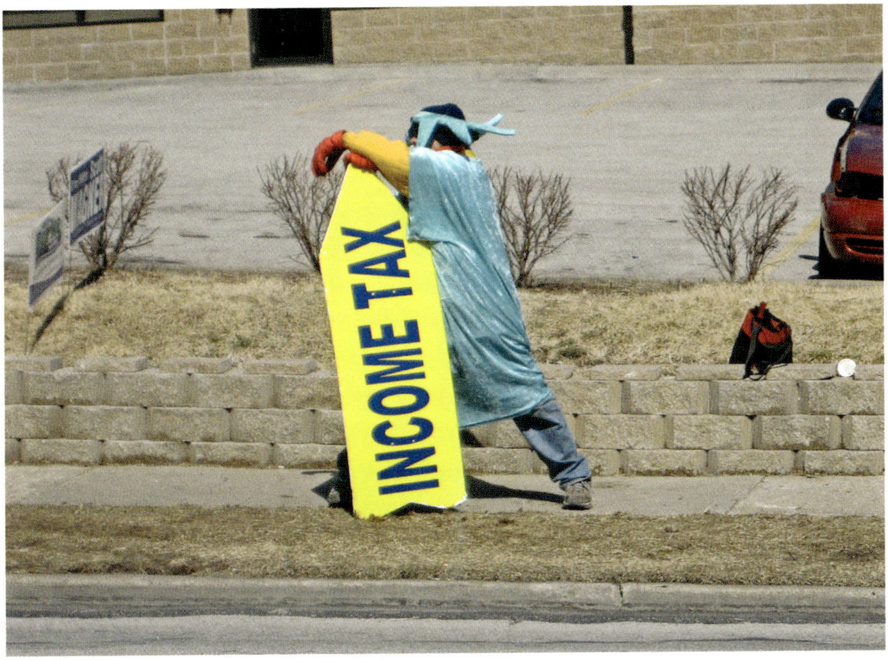

Liberty Leading The Traffic: Every April, Americans must pay their annual income tax, and in the months leading up to tax day it is common to see men and women dressed in cheap Statue of Liberty costumes, attempting to drum up business for accounting firms.

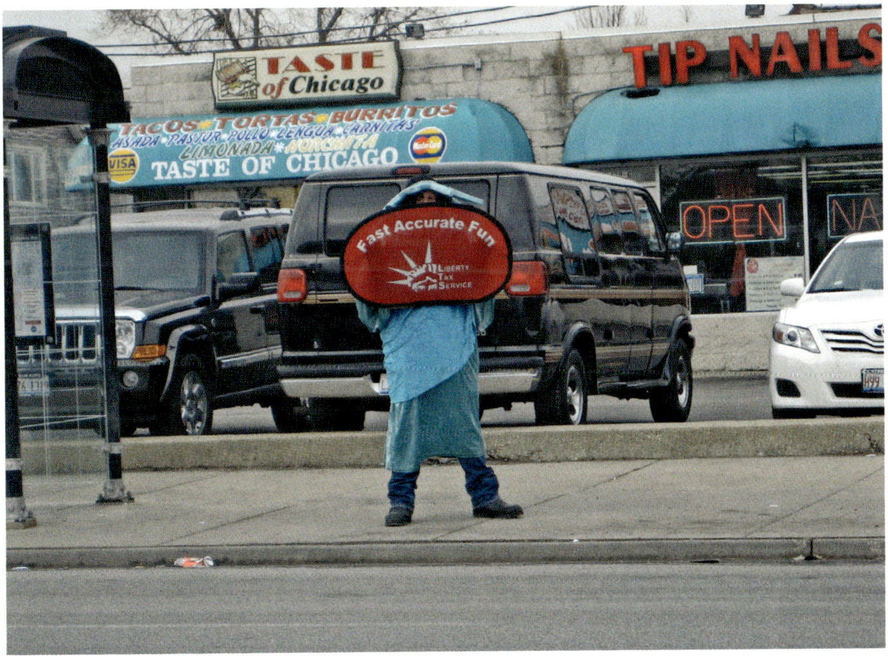

These photos of Lady Liberty, both depicted by young men wearing faux oxidized bronze suits and floppy foam crowns over their street clothes, were taken in Kansas City, Missouri (top) in March 2011 and Chicago, Illinois (bottom) in February 2012.

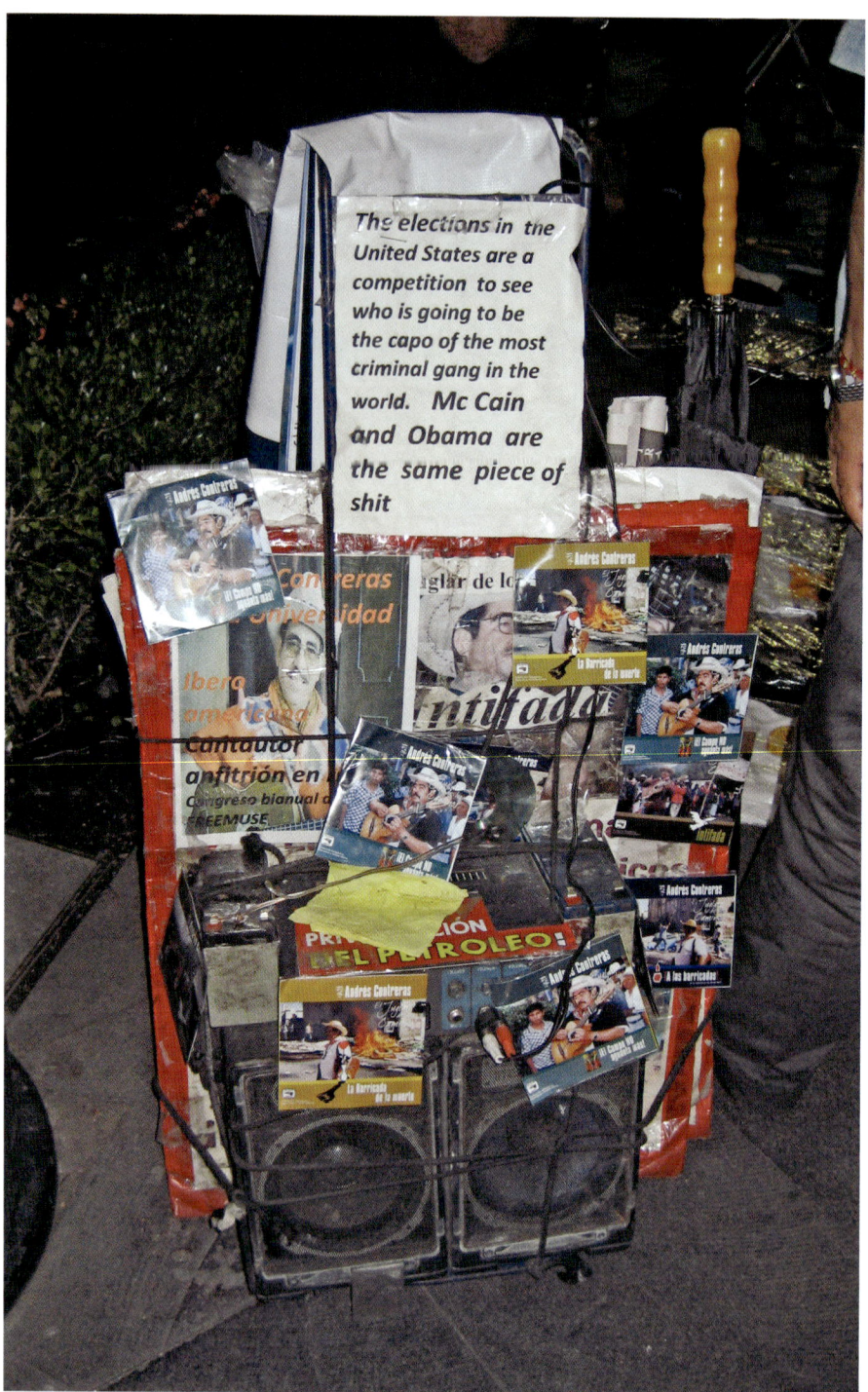

Music Vending Cart And Political Display With Speakers: This makeshift vending cart was pulled around the Zócalo. Music blared from its speakers while small laminated protest statements flipped down to display various sentiments to bystanders. Mexico City, 2008.

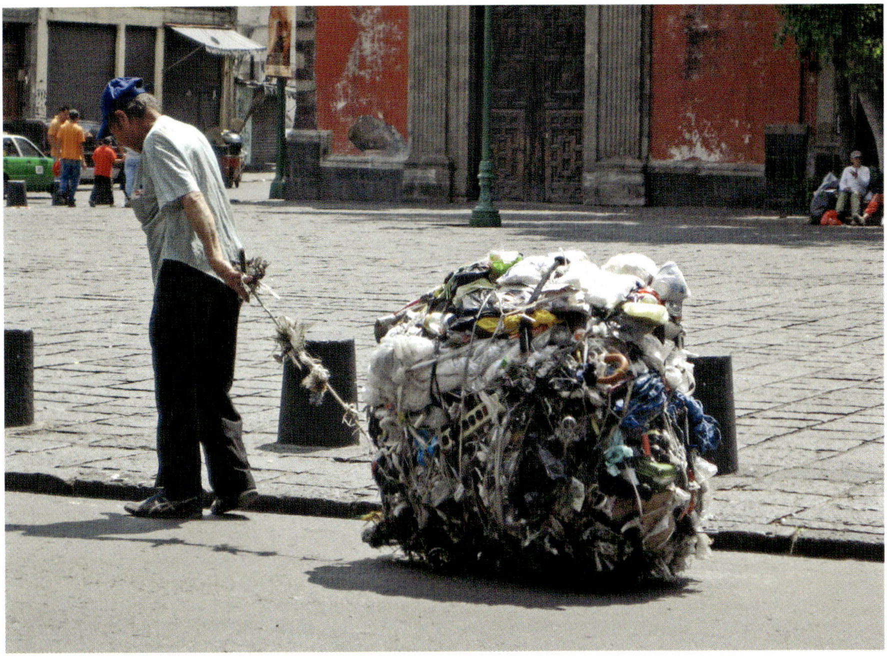

Ball Of Junk On Wheels: This tightly woven and heavy-looking mass of objects and cast off refuse is mounted on wheels that allow its owner to move it with relative ease from place to place. Mexico City, 2007.

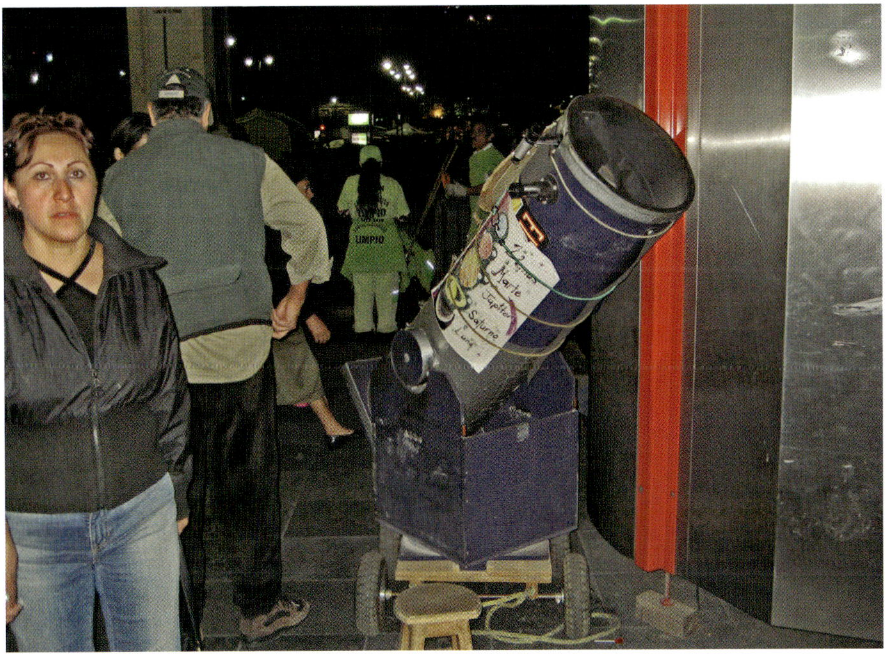

Mobile Observatory: For a small fee, a man in the Zócalo (main square) sells views from his high power telescope, mounted on a cart. A miniature seat is provided for comfortable viewing. A selection of illustrations of the planets is attached to the telescope. Mexico City, 2008.

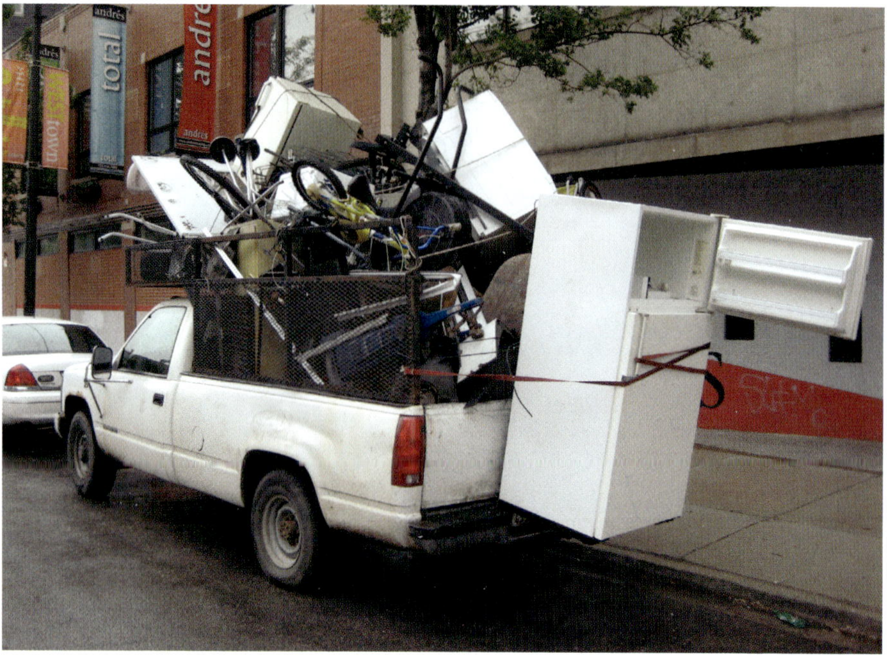

Chicago Scrapper Trucks: Day and night, scrappers in Chicago drive down the city's alleys looking for metal, furniture, and anything else that might have value as scrap or used goods for resale. Their trucks are commonly modified to hold massive amounts of material.

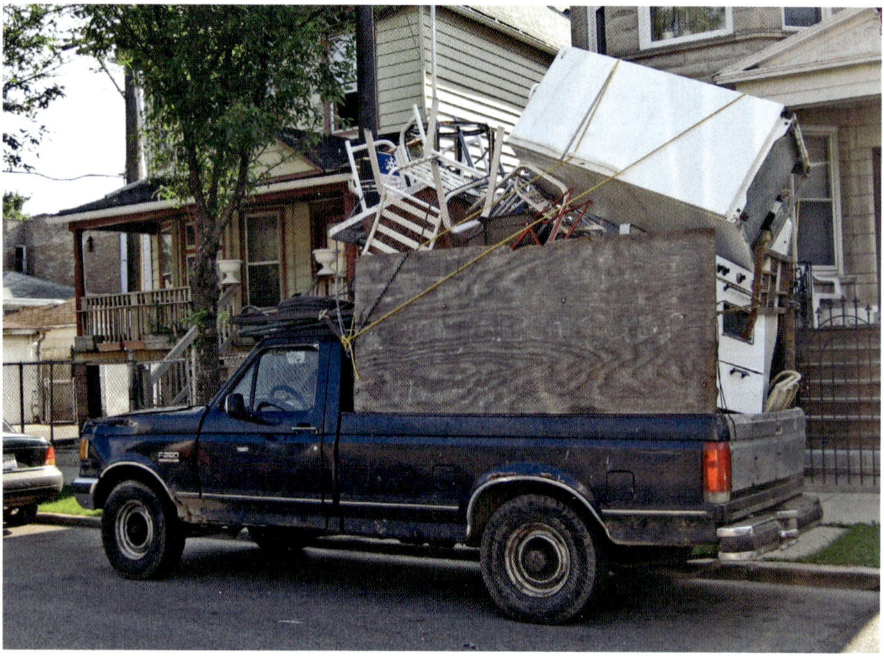

Due to the low value of many metals, tons must be collected in order to turn a profit, and the competition for these recyclables is fierce. Additionally, scrappers spend hours dismantling the items they find to separate the metal from the plastic, wood, or other valueless components.

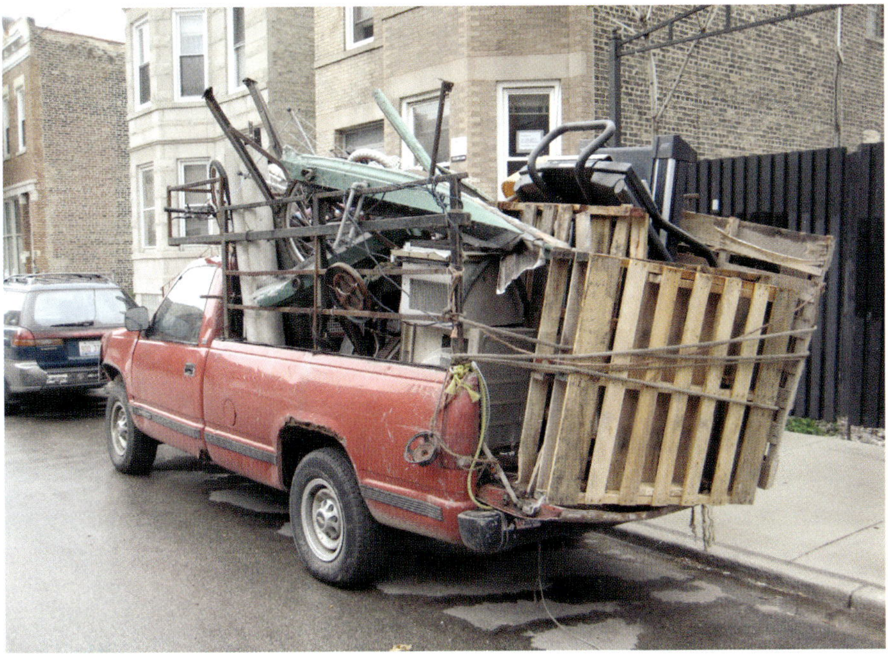

These photos were taken on Chicago's Northwest side in May and June, 2009. For an excellent and unusually sensitive study of this phenomena, check out the 2010 documentary *Scrappers* by Brian Ashby, Ben Kolak, Courtney Prokopas, Aaron Wickenden, and Frank Rosaly.

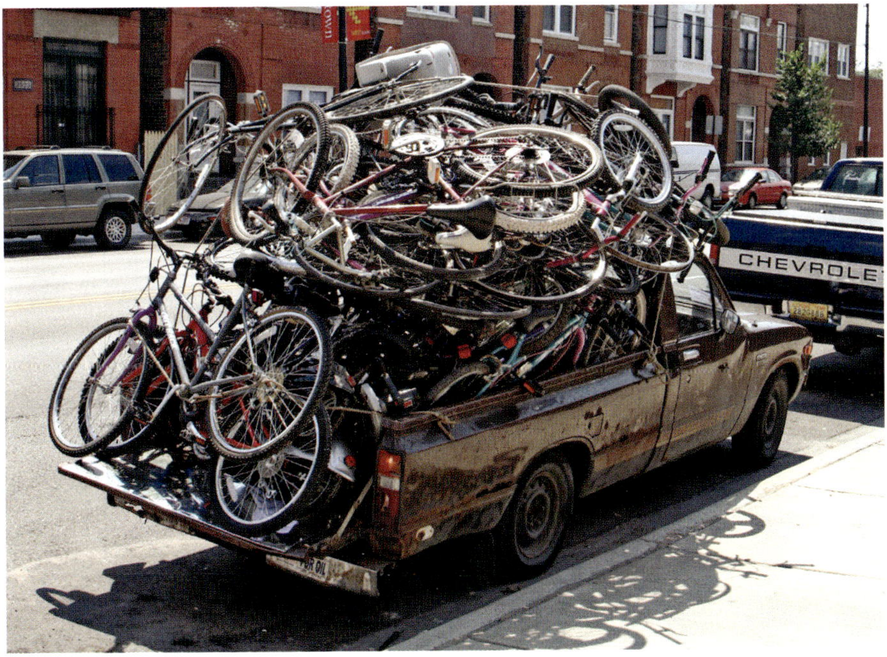

Truck Of Bikes: The Working Bikes Cooperative, "Diverts bicycles from the waste stream in Chicago by repairing them for sale and charity. Each year Working Bikes gives away over 5,000 bicycles locally and internationally." www.workingbikes.org. Chicago, July 2006.

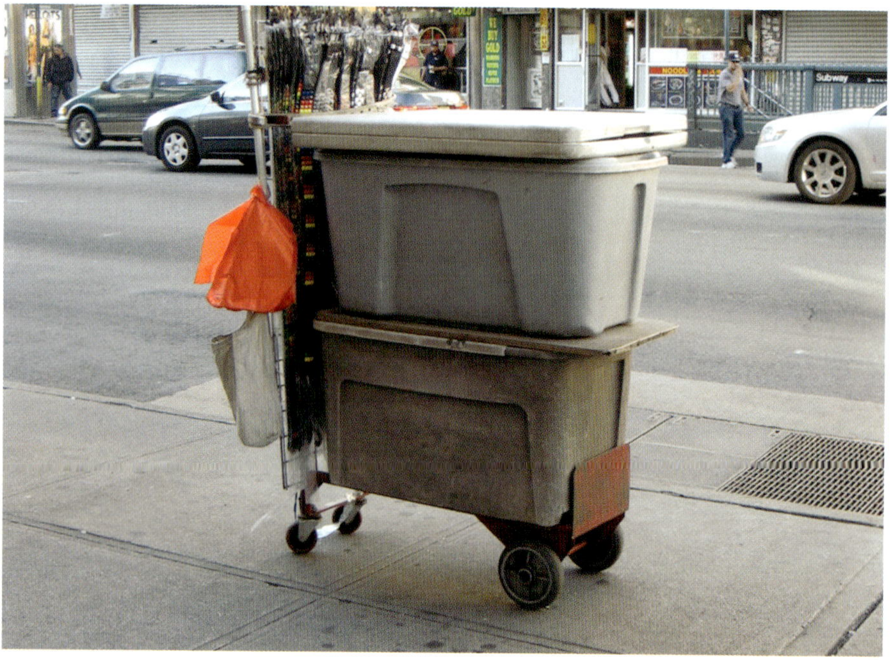

Tubs On Wheels: Everything this NYC dry goods vendor needs fits neatly on a four-wheeled dolly: a folding table, two plastic tubs of merchandise, a metal display rack (covered in merch), and more. Bright orange shopping bags for customers hang off the side. August 2010.

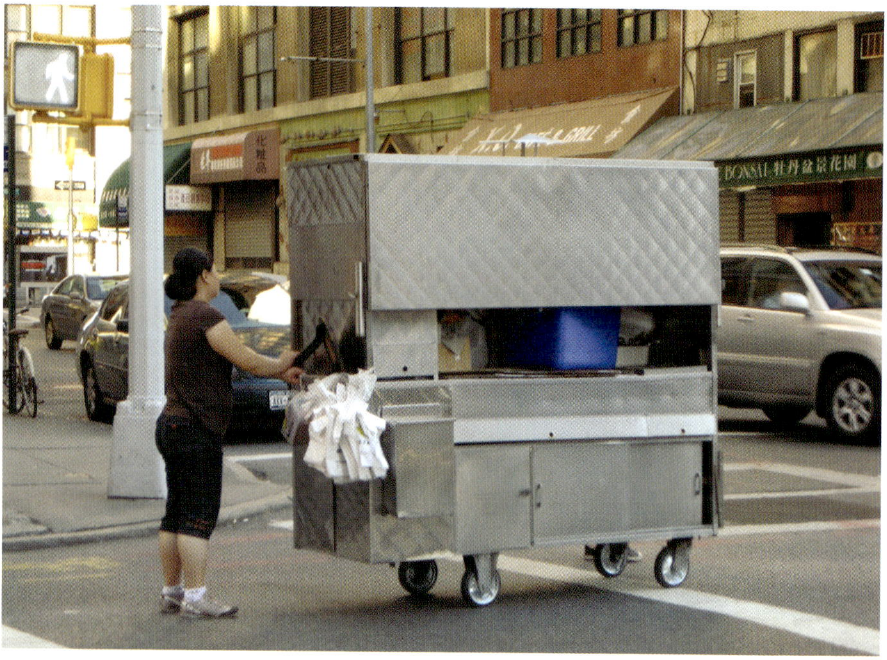

NYC Vending: New York has one of the most ubiquitous amounts of street vending in the USA. One sees all manner of both licensed and illegal vending carts and strategies. In this photo from August 2010, a woman pushes a typical food cart across the street in Manhattan.

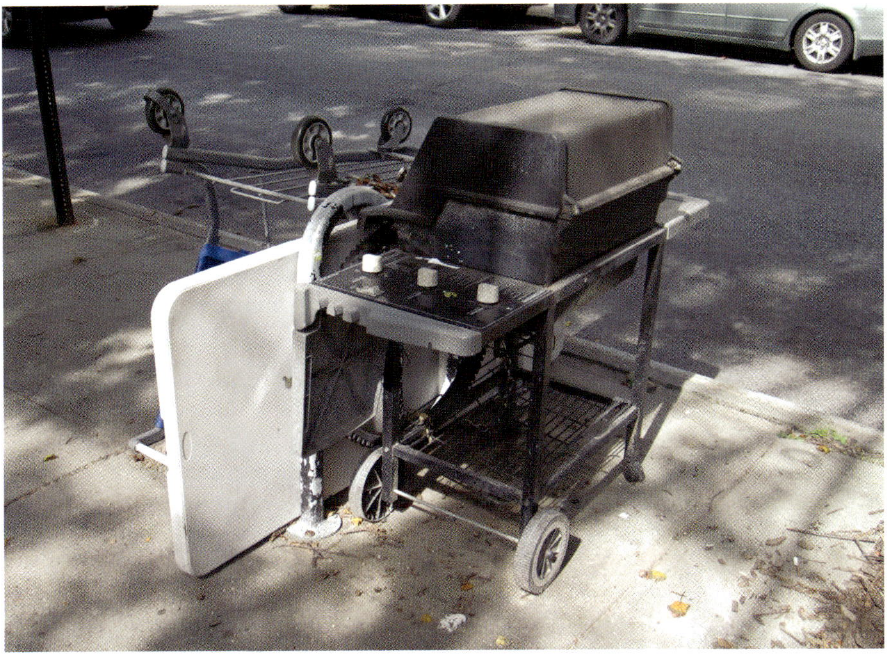

Instant Restaurant Or Serious Picnickers: A gas grill (without propane tanks), folding table and shopping cart were chained to a bike rack just next to Cuyler Gore Park in Fort Greene, Brooklyn, New York, 2011.

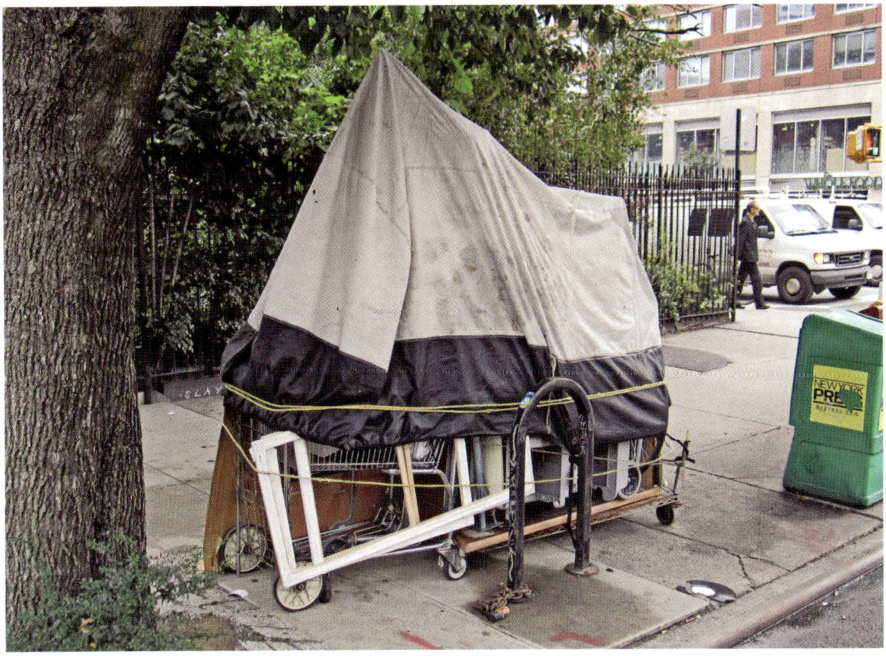

Public Vending And Storage: Many street vendors in New York leave their store's furniture in public wrapped up in a similar fashion to this one. This vendor's stall was located on the Lower East Side of Manhattan, New York, 2011.

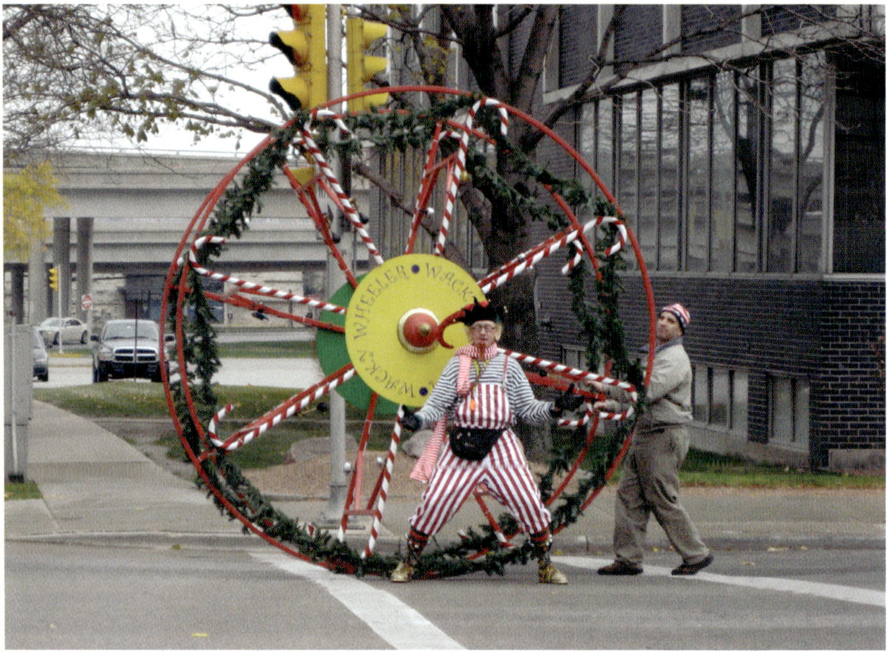

Human Hamster Wheel: This mobile spectacle, dubbed the Wacky Wheeler, was spotted early one weekend morning in downtown Milwaukee, Wisconsin. It's unclear if the Christmas decorations are used year-round, or were just in advance of the holiday. November 2007.

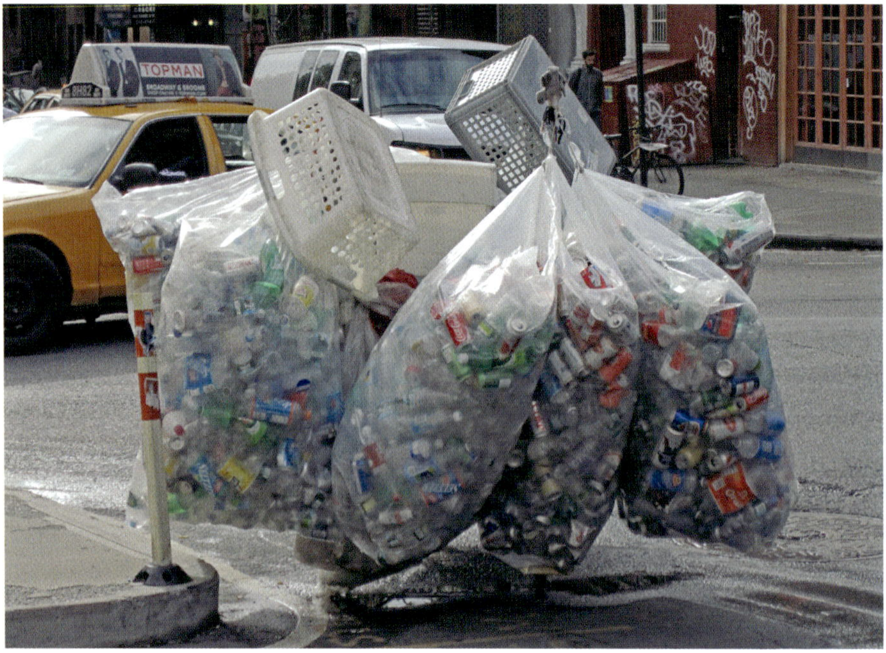

Looks Like Typical Street Recyling: This method of can collection, normally employed by unhoused persons, was part of a large, coordinated effort in the East Village and China Town. Many people used similar tools. We saw related on-street can sorting. New York, October 2011.

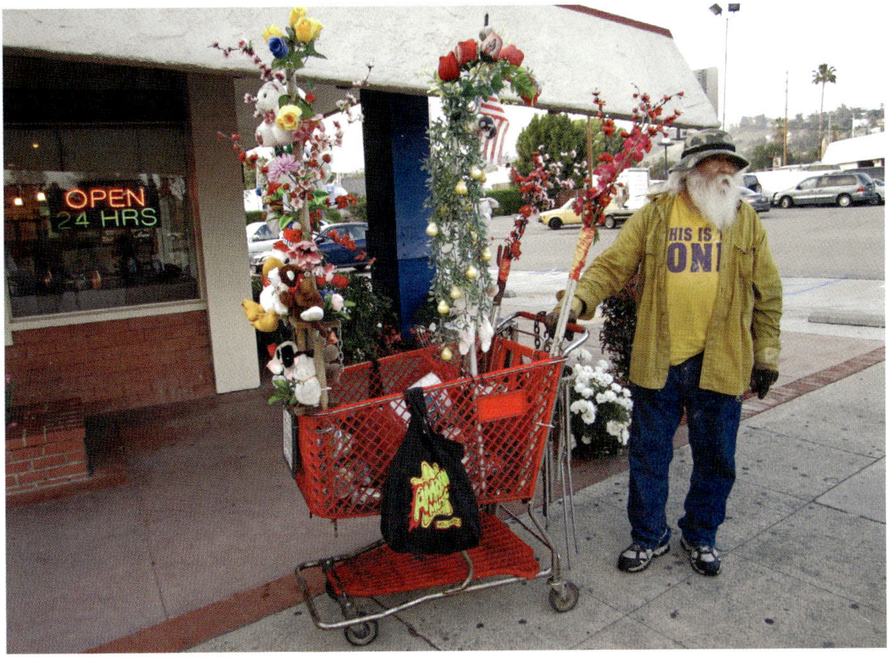

Advocacy With A Shopping Cart: Pedro Luis used to live on the street. He is happy that he now has a place to live, and to show his gratitude, he pushes his decorated cart around calling attention to the plight of people who are not as fortunate. Los Angeles, 2011.

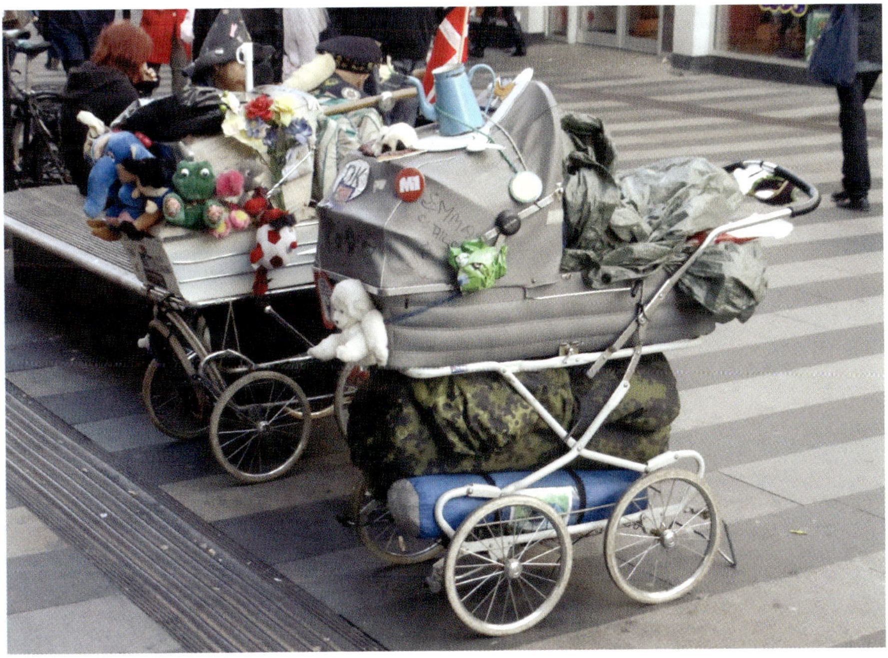

From Babies To Buskers: Here are two baby carriages converted to suit the mobile lives of the busker population in Denmark. These carts, which are common throughout Denmark, were photographed in the city of Århus, in northern Jutland, Denmark, in the fall of 2010.

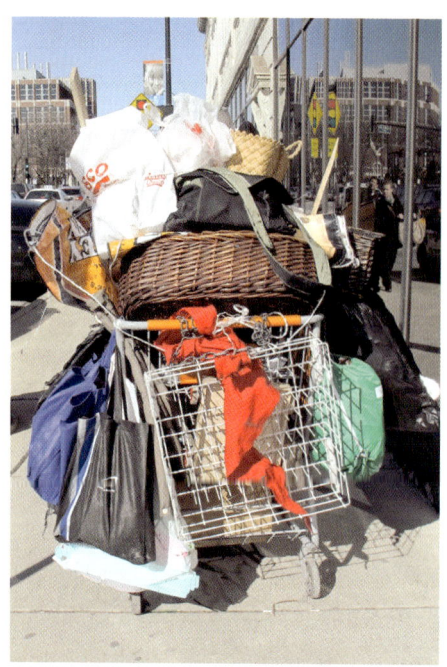
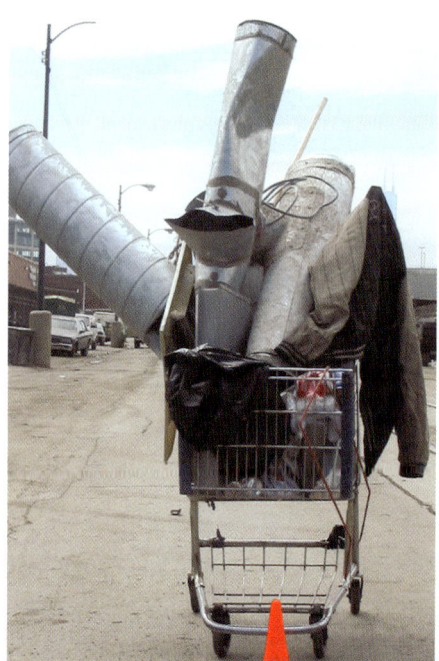

Photographs Of Shopping Carts Used By People On The Streets Of Chicago By Alexis Petroff: I began photographing shopping carts in 1999 during my daily bicycle commutes. I wanted to document the richness of the material culture, and the ingenuity and resourcefulness

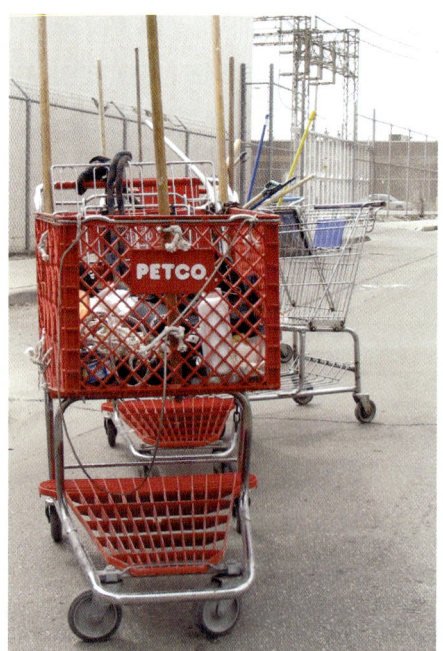
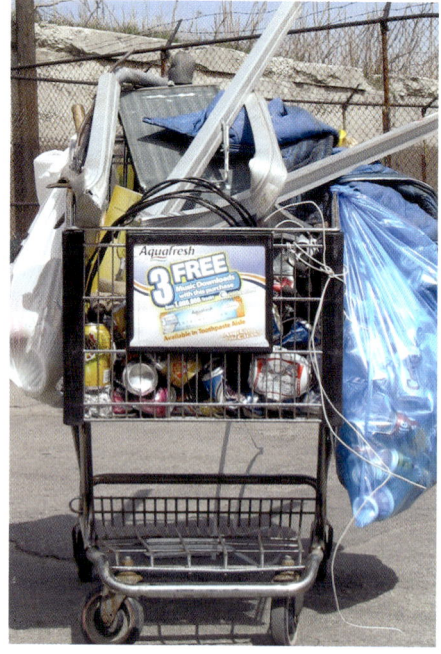

people use as they maximize hauling capacity of their carts by piling materials high as a sort of improvised, organized chaos. I want to show the material culture of alternative economies rather than portraits. The majority of carts I encounter while riding my bicycle in Chicago are

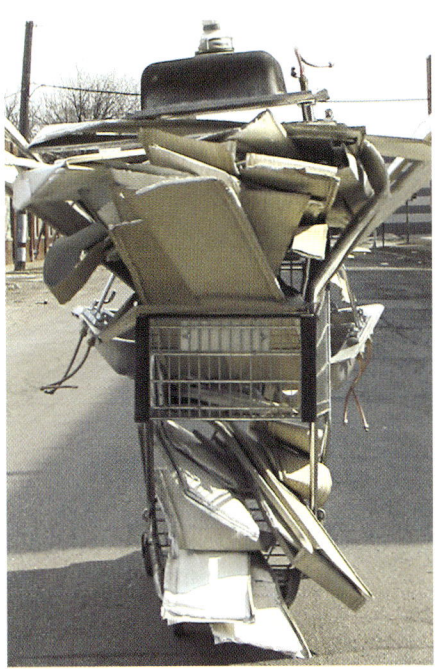 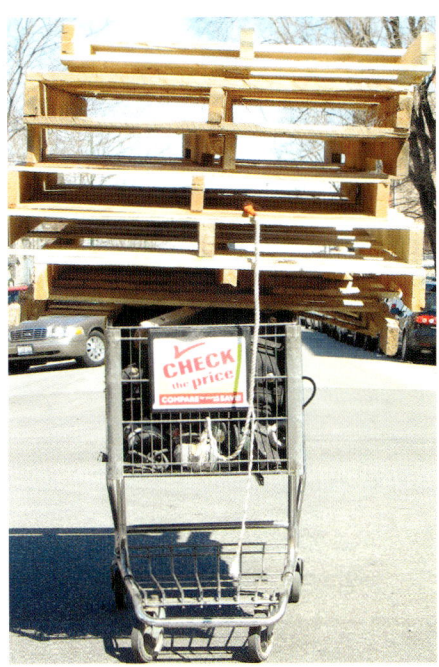

"working carts" used primarily for collecting items that can be recycled. Other carts are dual purposed and serve as recycling vehicles and nomadic living. While other carts carry only one's worldly belongings. Images page 38: (Clockwise from upper left) *Nomad*, 2012; *Duct*, Kings-

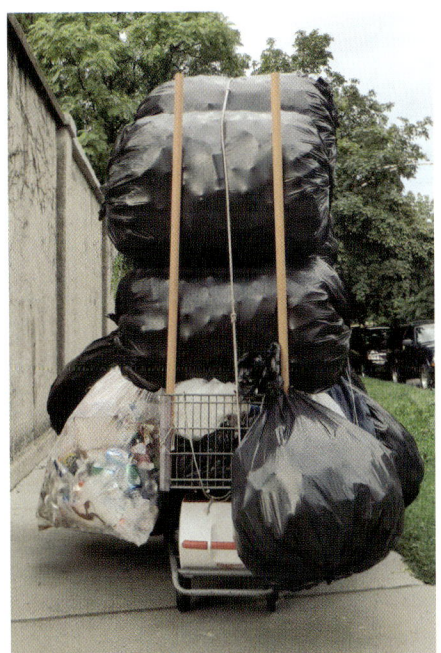 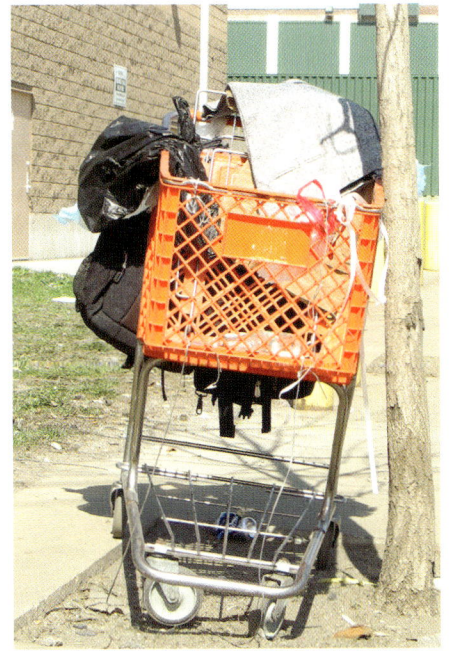

bury Street, 2006; *Brooms*, Kingsbury Street, 2006; *Cans +*, Hubbard Street, 2006. Images page 39: (Clockwise from upper left) *Sink*, Hubbard Street, 2006; *Pallets*, Ukranian Village, 2006; *Strapped*, Wrigleyville, 2012; *Rest*, Kingsbury Street, 2006.

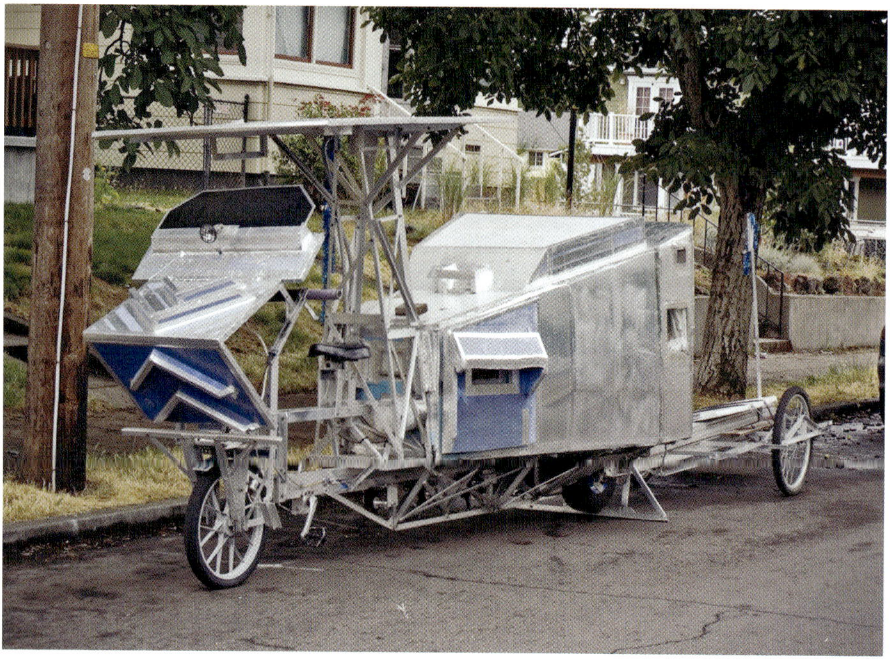

Brian Campbell's RV Bicycle: Brian Campbell is a bit of a West Coast legend in the United States. He has been spotted in cities from California to Oregon and is rumored to have taken his bike to Mexico. Campbell's incredible construction, that he appropriately calls a "bike ship,"

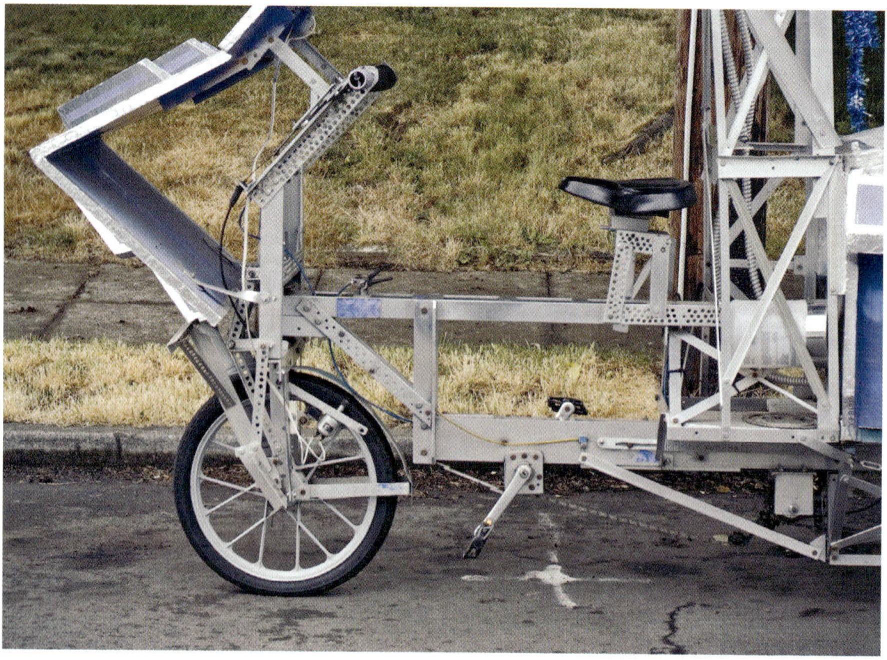

is a 100+-speed bicycle and mobile home. Campbell claims that the top speed of the bike is 70 mph downhill thanks to a special flywheel he designed. The bike ship is made from aluminum, modified bike parts, moped wheels, insulation foam, plus other ingenious material use.

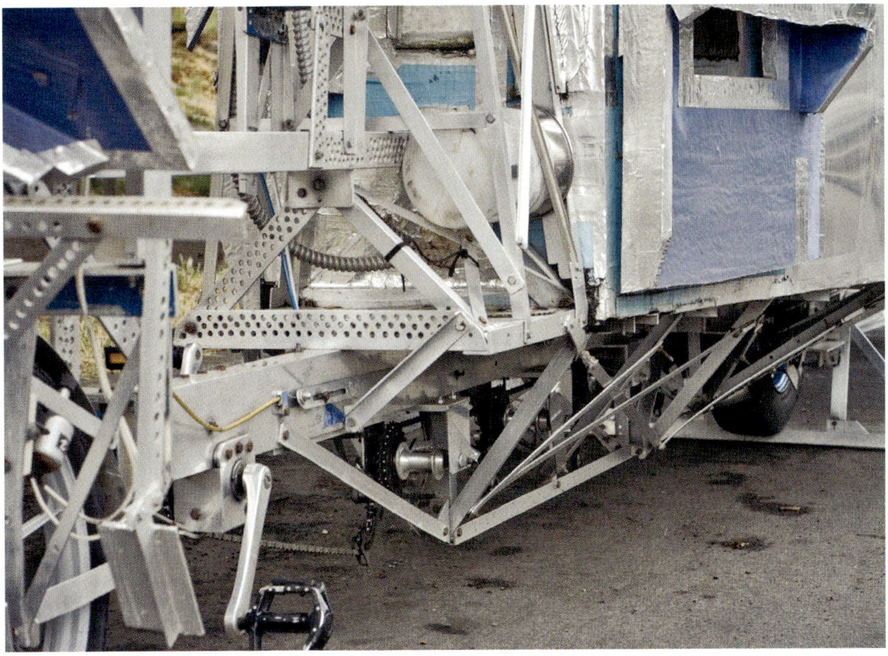

One person who talked with Campbell, Bob Crispas, described the bike: "[Campbell] said his design was inspired by the moon rovers and the moon landing vehicle, the super structure and the shiny panels. The interior was sweet too, looked comfy, and had a map holder and lots of

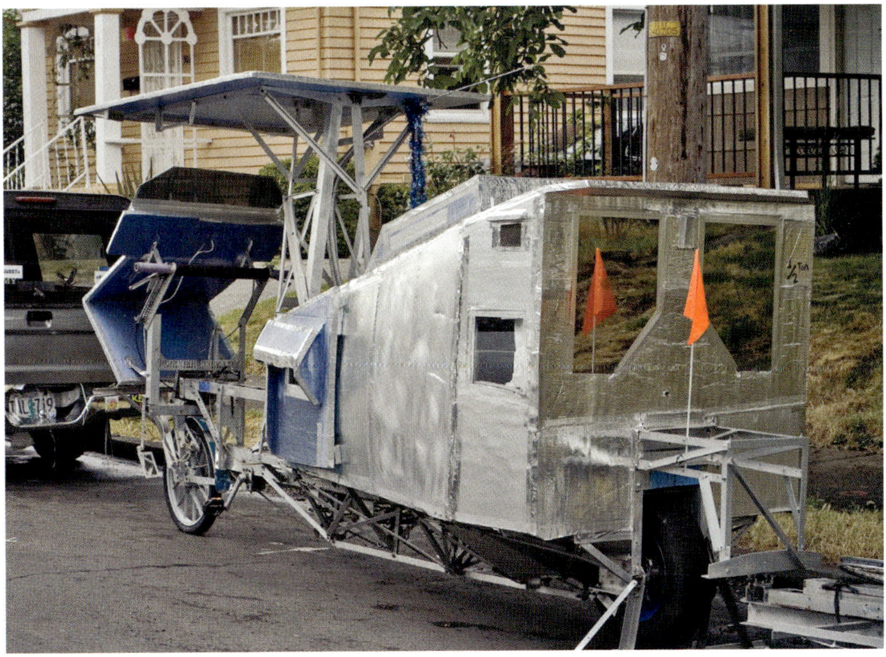

neat nooks and crannies to store stuff." Articles, photos and more information can be found at www.bikeportland.org. Information for these pages comes from an article Jonathan Maus wrote on the blog in 2009. These photographs were taken by Joseph Robertson, 2007.

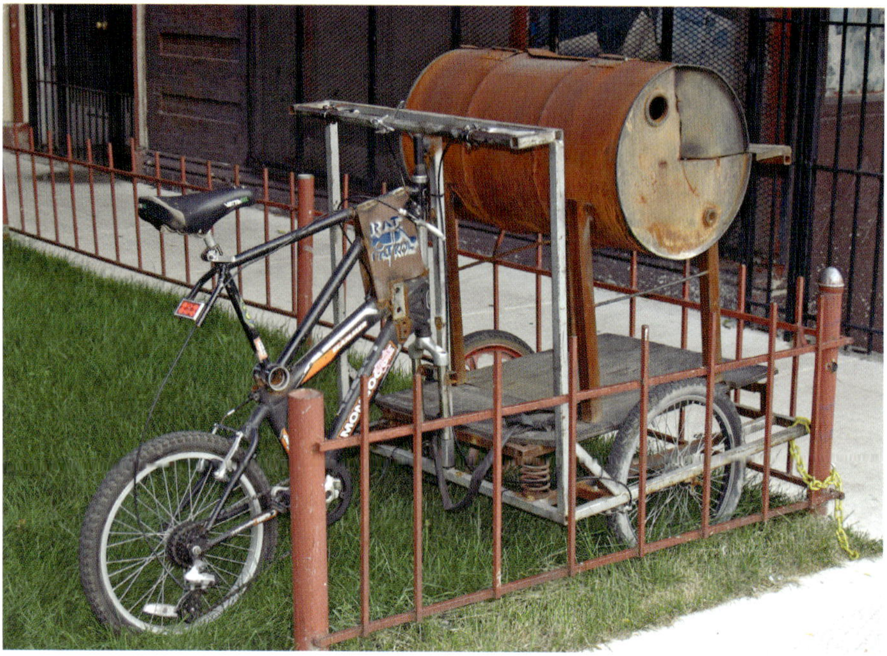

Mobile Grill: This vehicle is a combination of bike parts, an oil drum cut and converted into a grill, and other reused materials. It was designed by The Rat Patrol, a group of bike enthusiasts that makes many kinds of "Frankenbikes". Chicago, 2006.

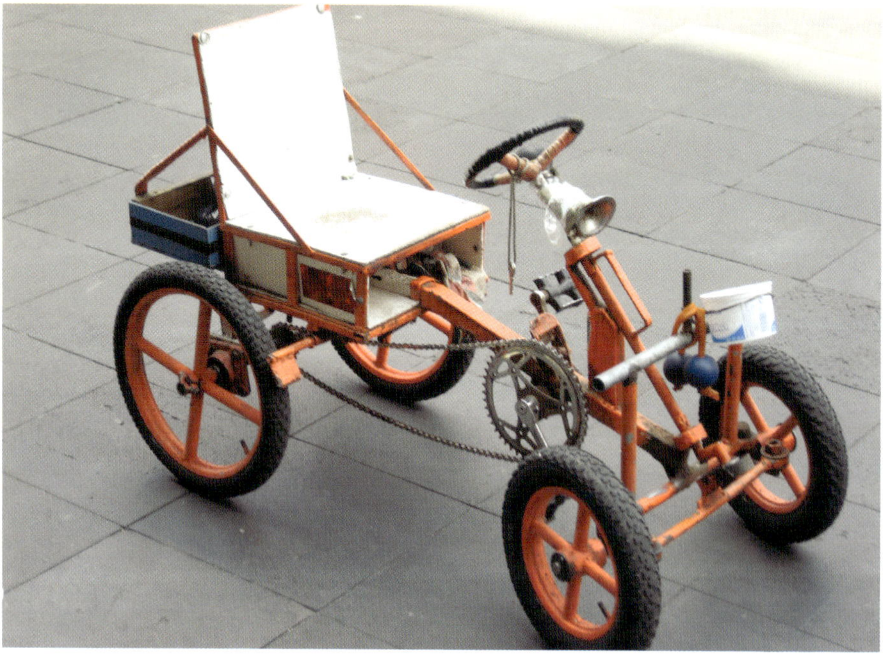

Single-Passenger Pedal-Powered Cart: This unique ride was photographed in Mexico City. The operator appeared to have a muscular disorder and this vehicle, that he was busy repairing, looked like his method of conquering those challenges with ingenuity and style. August 2008.

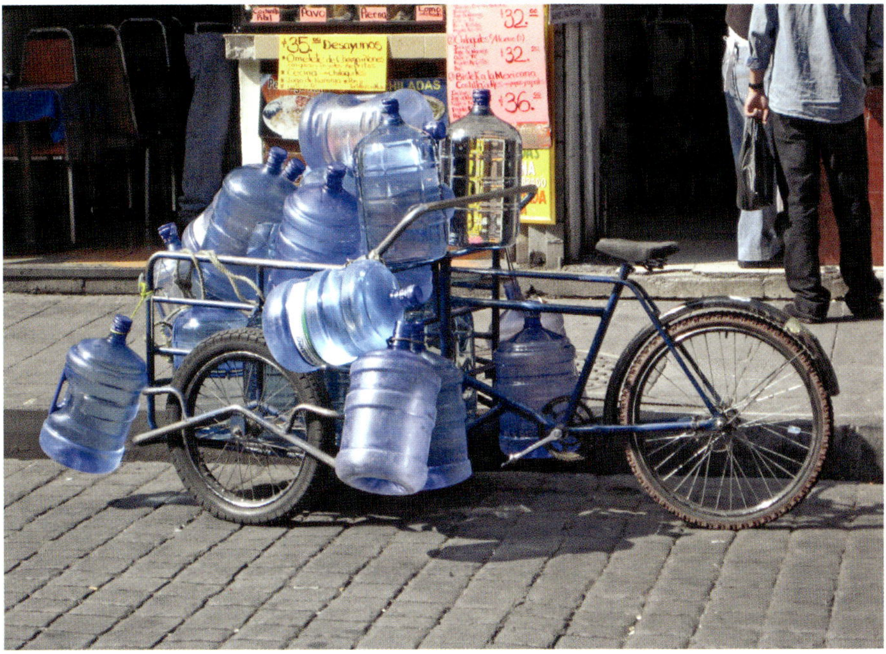

Watercycle: This oversize three-wheeled delivery bike was observed in Mexico City. Potable water is an everyday necessity in Mexico and this durable-looking vehicle appears to be capable of transporting many hundreds of pounds worth of filled water jugs. 2007.

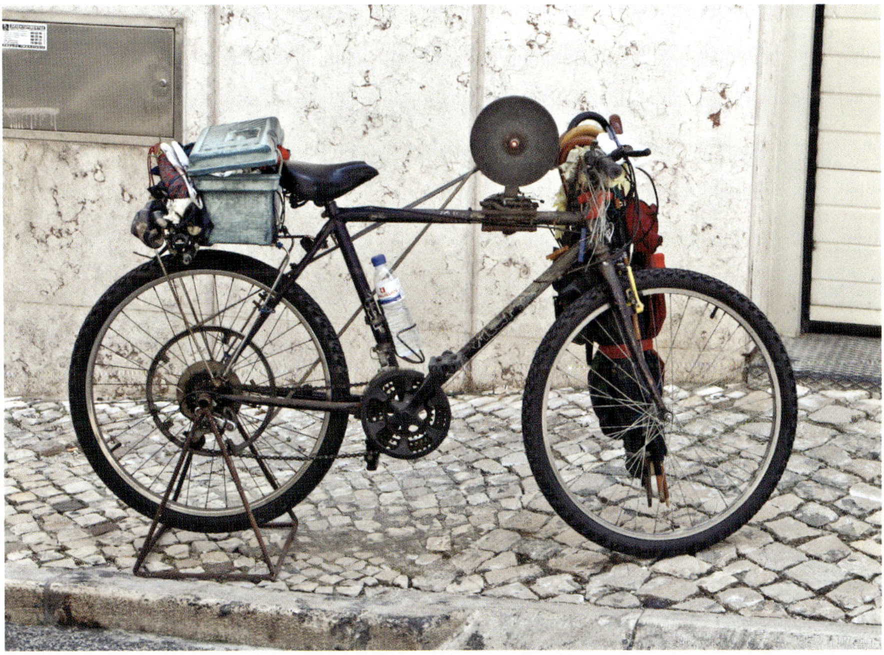

Pedal-Powered Knife Sharpening: This mobile service was used by a man parked outside of a restaurant. He came out with a bundle of kitchen knives, sharpened them outside on the street, brought them back in, and rode away. Taken in Lisbon, Portugal, May 2011.

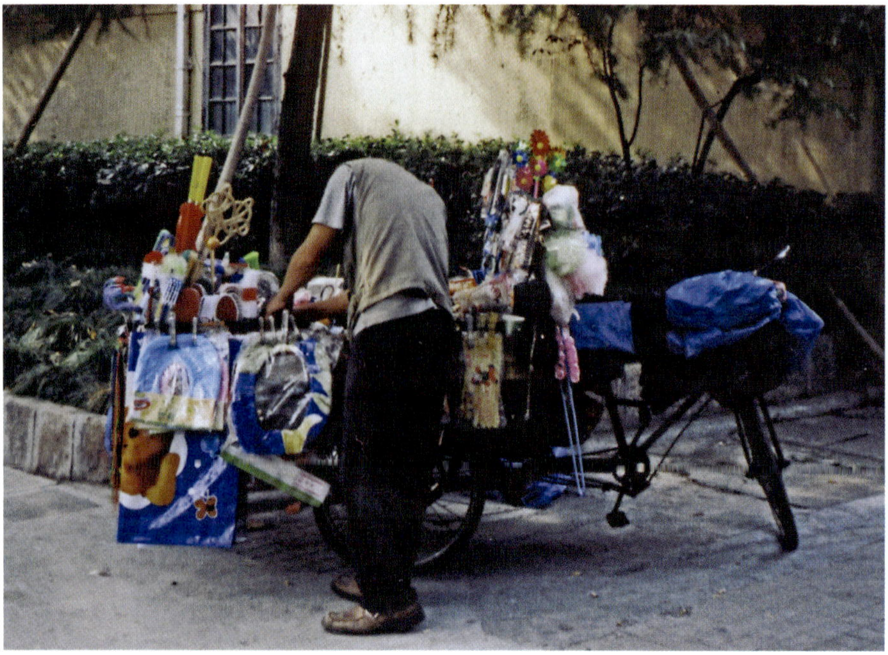

Transit And Then Some: Unlike the rural towns where portable shops are a necessity, Shanghai has thousands of stores selling everything imaginable. Bicycle-powered convenience stores, however, do a brisk neighborhood-based business. Bicycles provide both mobility and stability.

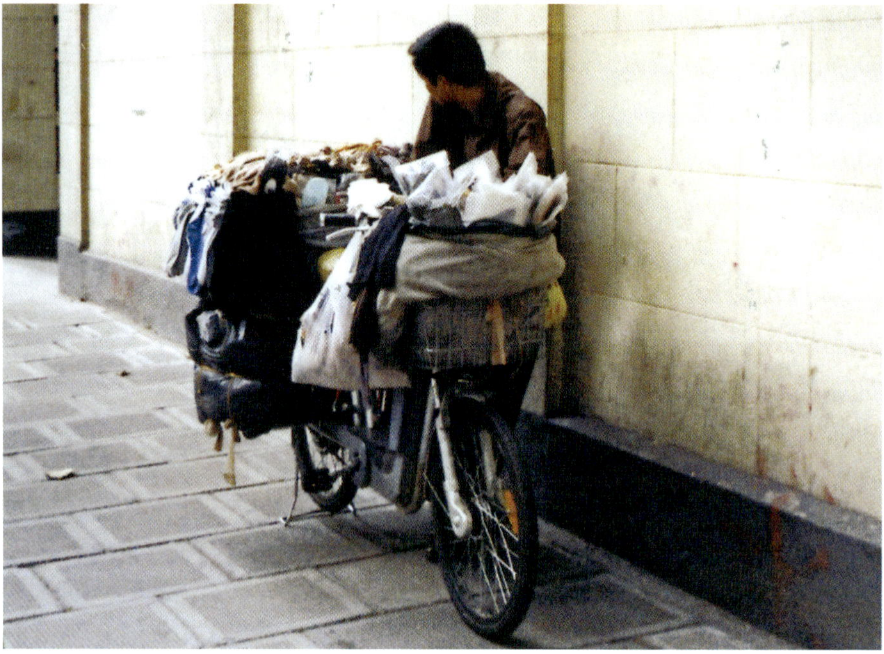

Who needs a sales counter when you have a solid double kickstand? Socks, undergarments, shoelaces, towels, and other necessities swiftly materialize at the entrance to any building, and just as swiftly disappear if needed. Photos taken in Shanghai by Jen Hofer, October 2008.

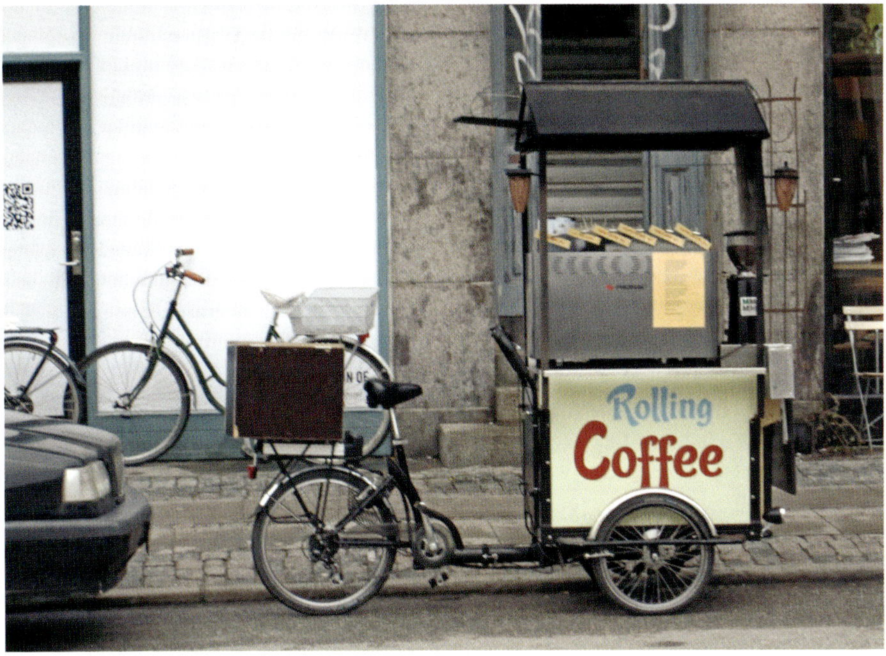

Restaurants On The Go: Copenhagen has a strong bike culture. Nearly 200,000 people commute to work each day in a metropolitan area of around 2 million. It makes a lot of sense that there are many additional uses for bicycles like a mobile coffee shop (top image) and a wheeled crêperie (bottom image). Both restaurants are built on what is called a Christiania bike. It is a three-wheeled bicycle with a box on the front that can be used for carrying people and a wide range of other things. They are a common sight around Copenhagen. Photos from 2011.

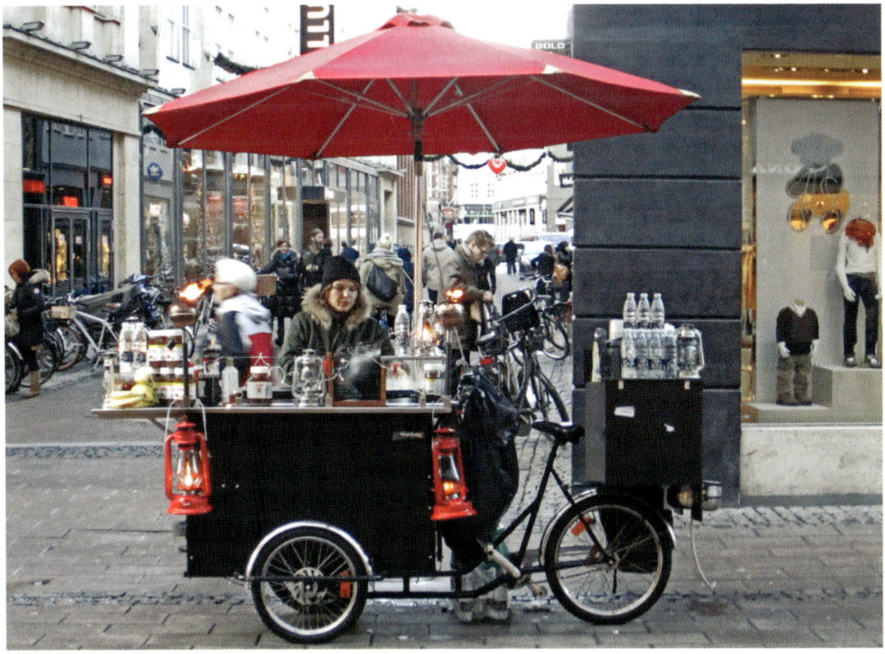

BAR BIKE

Christian Ettinger interviewed by Eric Steen

Colorado artist and beer fanatic, Eric Steen, visited Hopworks Urban Brewery in Portland, Oregon, to interview owner Christian Ettinger in December 2010. The conversation centers on the brewery's commitment to the environment, the famous "bar bike" that pops up around the city offering music and beer, and the conceptual stages of the "bar bike." Since the interview the "bar bike" has been built and is open for business.

Eric Steen (ES): How did you initially think to integrate bikes and beer, together, for Hopworks?

Christian Ettinger (CE): I mean, just for me personally, they've both been a big part of my life. So, I'm just always looking to surround myself with the things that I like. I got my first gear bike when I was thirteen, basically been riding them ever since. I had the BMX, of course, when I was like six through when I was twelve, and then I got my first mountain bike. That's what my friends and I did when we were thirteen and on, is we would just get on and ride.

ES: Yeah, so just two things that you love.

CE: Yeah, and I started homebrewing when I was eighteen, or nineteen I guess. So I've been making beer and riding bikes for longer than I haven't been. And I love them both dearly, so bringing those both together in a business plan that's sustainably based just seemed natural.

ES: That actually leads me to another question. Hopworks is an organic brewery and isn't it the United State's first carbon-neutral brewery?

CE: Yeah, it's harder to qualify internationally, but we're the only one in the U.S. and our carbon neutral certification company, or certifier, told us [we're the only one in] the world. But we're the only ones to make that commitment for our entire operation, not just for one beer, not all our beers, but our entire company. So we quantify upstream. There's five basic points in which carbon is consumed as, you know, a business. So if you take it cradle-to-cradle it's from basically the raw materials being extracted all the way to the end product being destroyed, recycle, upcycle, downcycle, whatever it would be.

Then, we do the cradle-to-gate, which is we've just done an assessment from the time the ingredients are extracted to the time the beer leaves the door here. So, three of the five points. Doing a downstream assessment

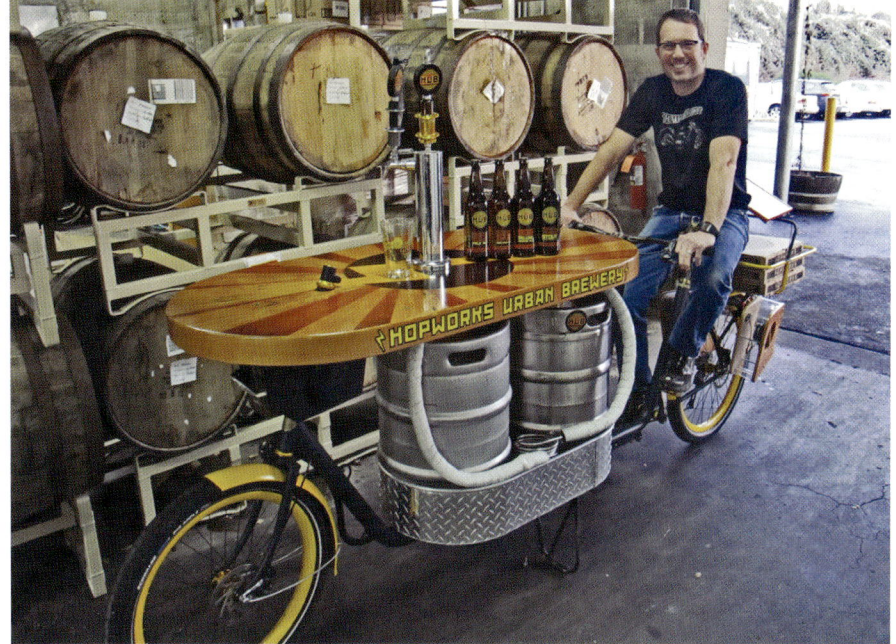

Bar Bike: Christian Ettinger of Hopworks Urban Brewery, Portland, Oregon, sitting atop the Bar Bike. Photo by Eric Steen, 2010.

is a little more loose because it's outside of your control. You're now distributing beer to a third party, then they're going to they're points of retail and then it goes from there to the consumer and then from there the bottles are recycled, the kegs come back, the liquid is filtered through the human body. It's a lot more nebulous down there. So we do cradle to gate and the 700 metric tons that we're responsible for, for consuming, about 120 to 130 of those are mopped up with our renewable energy credits with PGE's Green Mountain Program.

    The Green Mountain Program forces PGE to source the kilowatts that we consume renewably. Hydro, and solar, and wind. Mainly in this area it's hydro and wind. They can't source it from the Boardman Coal Powerplant, you know. The balance, about 560, 570 metric tons, is mopped up with these carbon credits effectively, but it's a very detailed analysis on the amount of energy we use and then that carbon that's consumed and basically emitted as a greenhouse gas. [That] is mopped up with an equal amount of reforestation that can sequester that carbon from the atmosphere and bring it back as plant food, to be available as tree-growth or whatever else nature does with it. It's basically reforestation in Colorado and Panama. That's the company we work with currently, it's ClearSky Climate Solutions. So, they're very much carbon credits, but we've taken a very deliberate step to be neutral in those three of five points, with the goal of being five when we're looking downstream as well. But we're only three years old, and being where we are I'm very proud of even taking that big step, you know.

ES: And you've even used recycled materials in your parking lot.

CE: Yeah. This table that your elbow is on is from our ceiling joist from the building. How beautiful is that, 1948? Feels good, looks good, and works well. I look at our renewable, not our renewable but our sustainable practices as being very dynamic, and the carbon-neutral part is just one part of what we do.

The other things are our organic initiatives: zero waste. All our beers are certified organic, half our produce is organic, all our proteins are hormone free, vegetarian fed and free range. And of course our energy – we're boiling our beer with Oregon made biofuel, biodiesel B99 so we're using Oregon made feedstock for the fuel for the kettle. And our energy efficiency upgrades, just got infrared fryers, we just went through a $7900 cooler upgrade on our 20x40 walk-in cooler and then our 10x14 upstairs that allow the compressor and evaporator to behave intelligently. Normally a cooler runs 24-7 basically, or the fans do at least, the compressor comes on when it needs it. [But] this allows everything to function in an optimal fashion, so they'll shut off. Basically what was just installed, they just took the data yesterday I guess, it saves thirty percent on a very big electrical load, which is refrigeration. So that's our most recent initiative.

The month before that we got our infrared fryers, which have thirty percent greater capacity and uses thirty percent less fuel than the previous ones that we had. So … our construction … we took the LEED template, you know Leaders in Energy and Environmental Design, took that template and bootstrapped it and did it ourselves, without getting any certification, but the principle being very genuine that we're just trying to reduce, reuse, recycle. We deconstructed the building, recycled the material that was unusable and reused every bit of it that we could to make our booths, to make our bookcases, to frame. We saved about a third of our frame material from reusing it. I mean the door casing around that door right there, that's all lumber from the site, you know. We just kept a big pile of it and kept picking away at it.

And then also in terms of construction, energy efficient lighting program in the production areas. I figure that if we have a very comprehensive plan then there are some guilty pleasures, and for us it's create a nice ambiance as well. So, we're just doing that dance everyday, trying to figure out what matters, what you can go without for a short period of time. Eventually we'll have a really nice expensive LED lighting system when the price comes down; you can see that LED lightbulbs have already dropped fifty percent in the last year. They were originally eighty bucks each, for one light bulb, and now they're about half that so you just kinda wait till you can afford it cuz if you overspend on it, you're out of business and you got eighty jobs that are gone and that doesn't do any good to anyone. So, you gotta be smart about it.

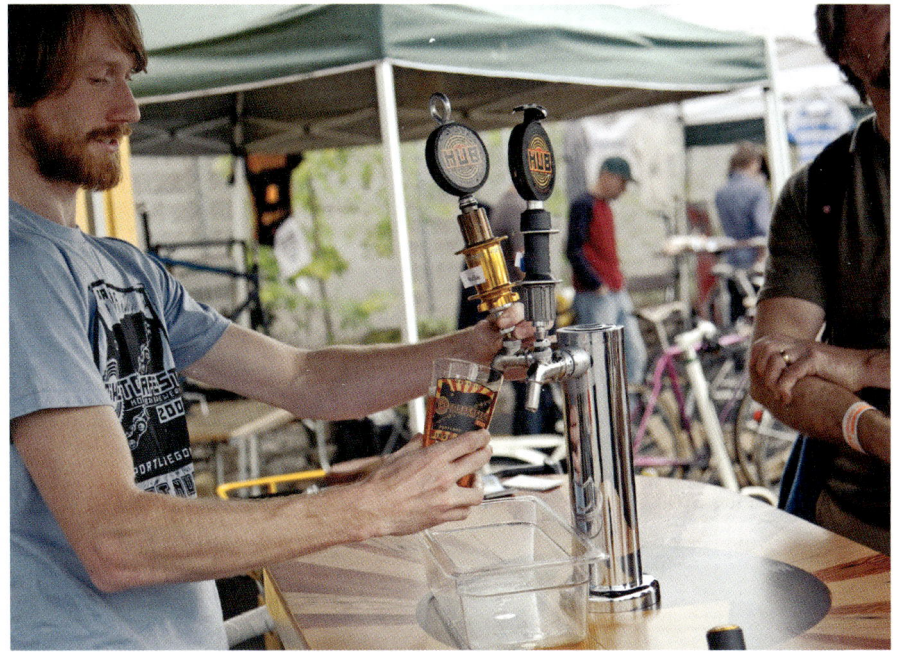

Bar Bike Beer Pour: Using the tap that is built into the bar bike to pull a pint. Photo by Tim LaBarge, 2010.

ES: Do you have someone on staff that is constantly looking at ways to reduce? Is that you?

CE: Yeah, it's me basically; I just challenge everybody to look at it through the same eyes, the same lens. Where are our opportunities to save power while minding the guests experience? Power and gas, and ultimately the guests' experience is what pays the bills so you gotta make sure that that's the paramount importance. If they're eating, they're eating and drinking world class food and beer, then everything else falls under less scrutiny I guess and if we've taken care to mop up most other things as well, then, the more layers of our onion they peel back the more satisfied they are that we're not just green washing, you know. That's my goal, to just make it a very genuine experience, we're just honest people making great food and great beer. They're having the opportunity to vote with their dollar, cuz the other businesses that aren't doing that are charging the same amount you know, should really be scrutinized. They should have an option so they get to vote with their dollar basically.

ES: When you say "genuine people" it reminds me of what you said earlier about bringing your two interests together, the beer and the bikes. It reminds me that you have this Hopworks Bar Bike, I call it a beer bike, and you call it a bar bike. Maybe tell me a little about what the Hopworks Bar Bike is and then also the various modifications on the bike that have been

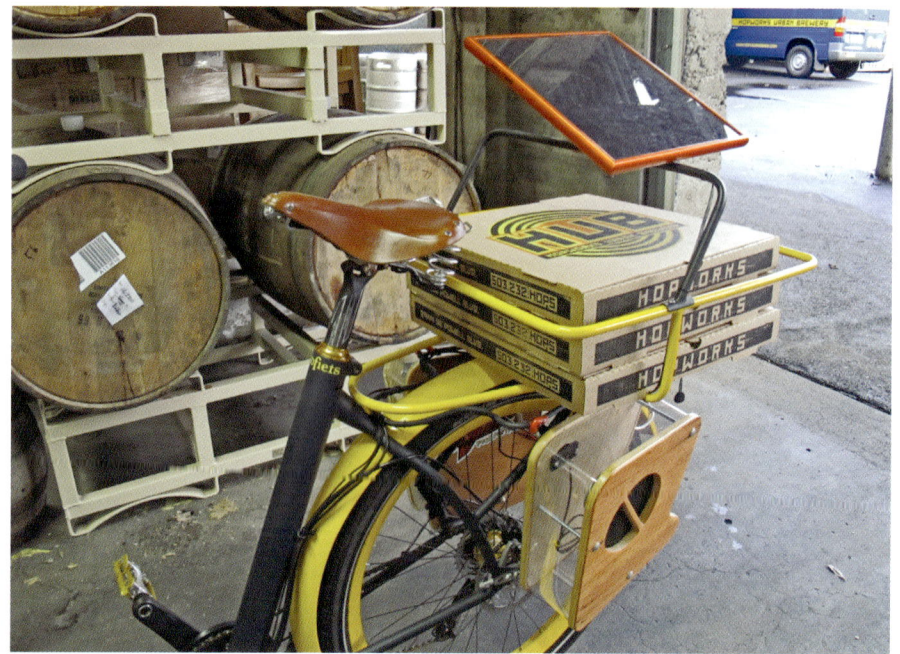

Detail Of The Bar Bike: The bike has a solar panel for powering a sound system. Pictured is one of the bike's speakers, and a yellow rack for holding several boxes of pizza. Photo by Eric Steen, 2010.

required to make it do what it does.

CE: Yeah, yeah, so I kind of came across MetroFiets, Jaime and Phil over there. So, BackFiets is the Dutch version that means "minivan" very literally and so they adapted the Dutch design to basically produce the same cargo bike, the same style, in Portland. So, rather than importing it, they're making 'em here, and it's very similar and very very cool. We basically ... they wanted to build a keg-hauler and I kinda wanted to build a mobile bar. I wanted to bring as much of a part of the party to one place that was possible. That was like bringing food, music, and beer altogether and that's effectively what it is, it is a mobile bar, five foot bar top made with the same old growth lumber that you're leaning against right now. Those veneers were laid out very artistically on a computer to bring our logos, it's got a lightning bolt running through it, radio looks like the sun, so the bar top is super cool. It has a draft pour with two taps, one's [made with parts from] Shimano, one's Chriskenny, you get your choice of flavors. There's a jockey, basically the frame was stretched and the cargo boxes were replaced with a keg pan. That's about eight inches deep and has two coils that are in the figure eight of the kegs, so you have two half barrel kegs and two coils, so it's a jockey box effectively, a draft-beer dispense mechanism that keeps the beer cold and pours a great pint.

ES: And so we're looking at 250 pints or something then right?

CE: Um, yeah basically, 248 exactly. Three large pizzas in the rear rack and in the canopy of that rear rack is a five watt solar panel that feeds power to the motorcycle battery that's in one of the panniers, so there's three speakers on it, one in each of the panniers and then one under the bar top that are fired off the motorcycle battery and a guitar amp that will take a signal from an mp3 player. And then the five watt panel just trickle charges the battery. So you got music, food, and beer. And it's brought to the party in the most renewable fashion possible, two legs, you know. I try to ride it where we can, you know. If it has to go more than five miles, we'll truck it there.

ES: How often do you get to take it out?

CE: Well, we had one event last week. Winter time, you know, it slows down quite a bit. Summer time, I mean there was one week in the summer where we used it five days in a row. It just totally depends on [the weather]. Oregon Craft Beer Month is July, so July is just really off the chain. We offer it up and as people find out about it they ask about it more and more

ES: So people hire the service or something?

CE: Well no, last week there was a party down here for a bicycle helmet manufacturer, their headquarters is down here on 12th and Division so I just rode it down there. Amelia met me with the kegs and we set it up and they had three hundred people there. We burned through two kegs. We'll do it for private functions as long as it's consistent with our philosophy, if they're environmental groups or bike groups or anything in those kind of worlds, you know. We try and be generous with it, we don't charge for it, we just want people to enjoy it.

ES: That's awesome! That would be so cool to throw a party and have you show up.

CE: Yeah, but unfortunately, we … Oregon state law is a little conservative so we can't actually, we can deliver beer to festivals and things like that but private parties we have to have an actual party host get the kegs, and meet us there. We basically set it up as a service but we never, we don't have possession of the beer at that point for private parties.

ES: Sometimes you actually carry the kegs out on the bike?

CE: I try not to. Yeah, it's too heavy and the frame can't handle it. We had one full keg on it once, and the guy who built it tipped it over. It's too top-heavy. You can handle two quarter barrel kegs, but really the bike's not meant to carry that kind of weight. When it's static on it's center stand, it's fine. But in transit man, you'd just smoke your breaks you know. It's got six inch rotors, we should probably put like eight inch downhill mountain bike rotors on it because it needs more help stopping. Any weight on it, even if it's just the bike it still wants to push through stop signs, even with hydrolic disc brakes.

ES: Do you see the Bar Bike being more of an everyday thing in the future, or do you want it to be this special thing?

CE: I want to build another one. Mountain bike based, that's something that I ... well, we have too many projects going on right now though, so I may have to push that off – maybe till we get this new pub open.

ES: But you're an entrepreneur, you can handle all that. [Laughter]

CE: Yeah I know. I love that. I was looking at email yesterday, I've got some good contacts, just trying to find the right company to try to help us build that but the way this Bar Bike #1 shot around the world on the internet. I should have done a You Tube page; it was probably a lost opportunity, could have had a million hits by now. But we're going to build another one, I would like to have that done this year, but on a mountain bike frame so that we can put Cornelius cans on it. It would be like five-gallon kegs [instead of the current fifteen gallons per keg]. I learned some stuff about it; it would definitely make it more flexible, easier to ride and you could probably get it set up to offer a whole different set of events, being an off-road bike.

ES: Would you have those five-gallon kegs laying down flat or something?

CE: When I was in Peru I remember seeing these motorcycle propane haulers that were motorcycle-based so they could use whatever they were – twenty, thirty pound propane bottles in panniers on the back of the motorcycle – and they could get down narrow dirt alleys and they could get to distant areas and dirt roads where cars couldn't get to. I was kind of inspired by that for the next design. To make more of a pannier-based five-gallon system that would be fully suspended. It might be a good project for a bike manufacturing company that has good engineering capacity, where it's not so much the intuitive design stuff but really truly engineered for that purpose.

MOBILE PROTEST

Disparate elements come into play while changing or questioning the status quo. Incorporating playful approaches can attract like-minded people to the given cause, as well as smooth out potential moments of friction and tension between participants.

A seriousness of purpose is also apparent in the kinds of projects and actions that we have categorized as Mobile Protest. The messages and content are clear. The delivery of these messages is made more accessible through the mobility of these situations: we are coming to tell you about something and potentially change your mind. Whether they are a system for amplification of voices or sounds, a vehicle that serves both ice cream and propaganda, or a crate that transports a man to freedom, these projects often live in multiple worlds of interpretation while they are in action.

Planning for and creating dissent and dialogue, whether it is in corrupt political systems or in shared city spaces, requires flexibility and innovation. This section highlights a few projects and examples of mobile phenomena that serve as tools for protest. Whether spontaneously assembled or meticulously executed, these mobile phenomena are all strong additions to the growing movements that they serve.

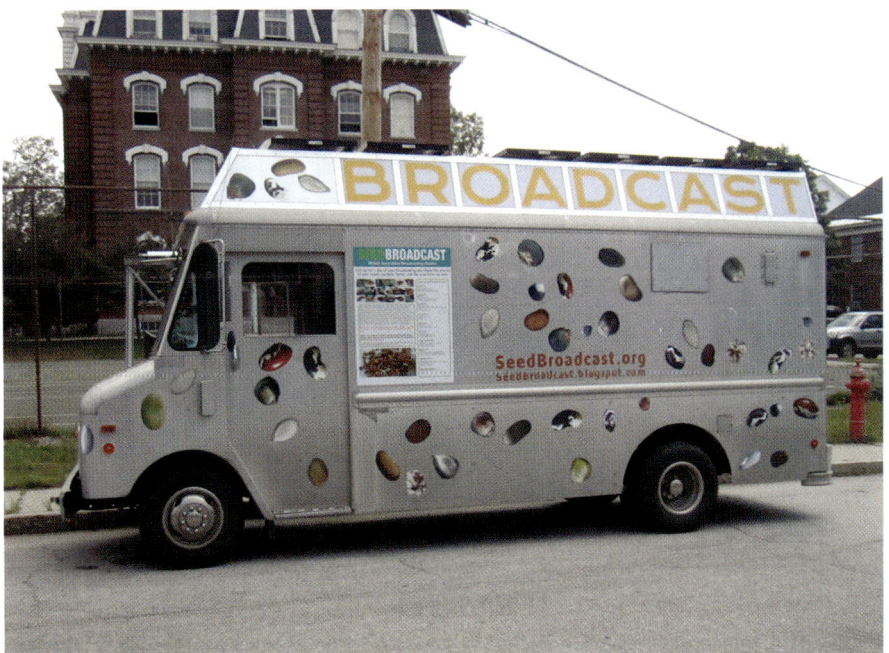

SeedBroadcast Mobile Seed Story Broadcasting Station: Touring seed libraries, gardens, farms, fields and streets of the commons, broadcasting grassroots voices of seed and food sovereignty. seedbroadcast.blogspot.com. Montepelier, Vermont. Photo by Bonnie Fortune, 2012.

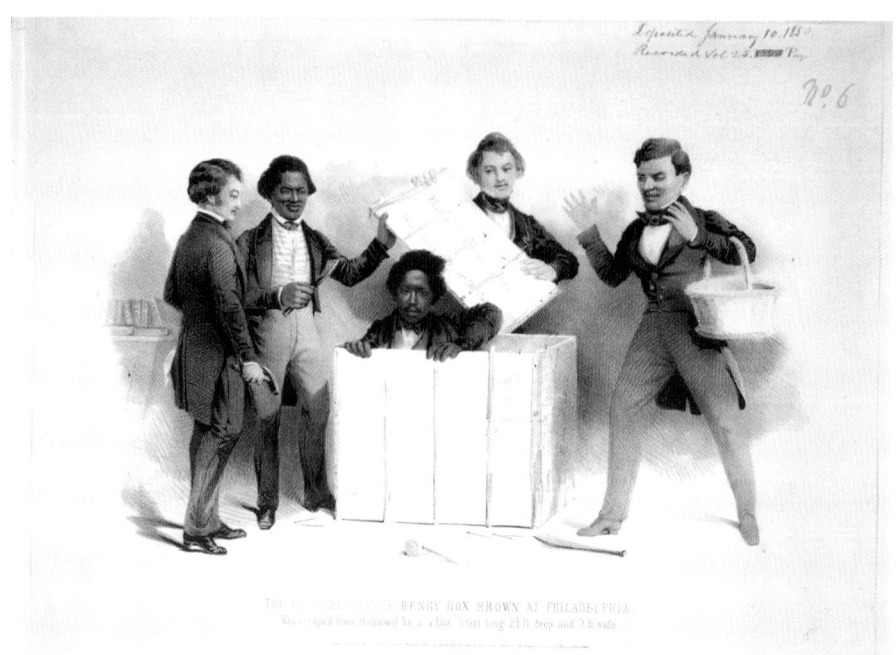

Ship Yourself To Freedom: "The Resurrection of Henry Box Brown at Philadelphia. Who escaped from Richmond Va. in a Box 3 feet long 2 1/2 ft deep and 2 ft wide." Lithograph by Samuel W. Rowse, 1850. Library of Congress Prints and Photographs Division, Washington, D.C.

The story of Henry "Box" Brown is one of radical social mobility that has inspired us for years. Brown was born into slavery in the 19th century in the southern U.S. state of Virginia. In 1849, through a tremendous act of both desperation and bravery, he packed himself in a wooden shipping crate and mailed himself to freedom from Virginia to Philadelphia, where he was received by members of the Philadelphia Vigilance Committee, an abolitionist group. The trip took over twenty-four hours of travel by wagon, train, and truck. Brown stayed still enough inside the crate throughout the entire trip to not alert the delivery and railroad workers of his presence.

When news got out about what Brown had done, he became an instant celebrity and traveled around telling his story, eventually moving to England after the passing of the Fugitive Slave Law of 1850 that would serve to return him to his oppressors. His act of bravery served as a powerful narrative in the abolitionist cause to get rid of slavery.

Brown did not wait to be liberated or for his oppressors to treat him with the dignity he deserved. He took direct action to solve the problem. Readers today will most certainly draw connections between Brown's story and the many tragic attempts that people have made to come into the United States via shipping containers or hidden within vehicles. We include Brown's story in the Mobile Protest section as a reminder of the great stakes that come with all kinds of mobility and an inspiration of what can be possible even under the most dire of circumstances.

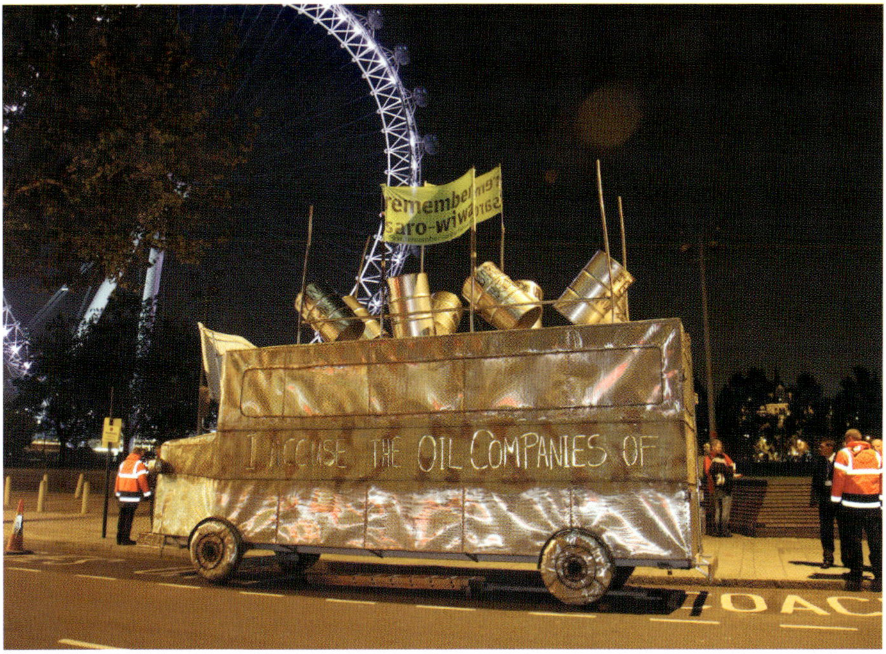

Remember Saro-Wiwa: Platform collaborated with others to create a living memorial to the Ogoni writer and activist Ken Saro-Wiwa and eight others who were executed by the Nigerian military government in November of 1995. British-Nigerian artist Sokari Douglas-Camp CBE created this life-size steel bus featuring the names of the Ogoni 9, and a quote from Saro-Wiwa: "I accuse the oil companies of practising genocide against the Ogoni." It traveled around the U.K. starting in 2005. Photos: (top) Martin LeSanto-Smith, 2008; (bottom) Ken Brown, 2011.

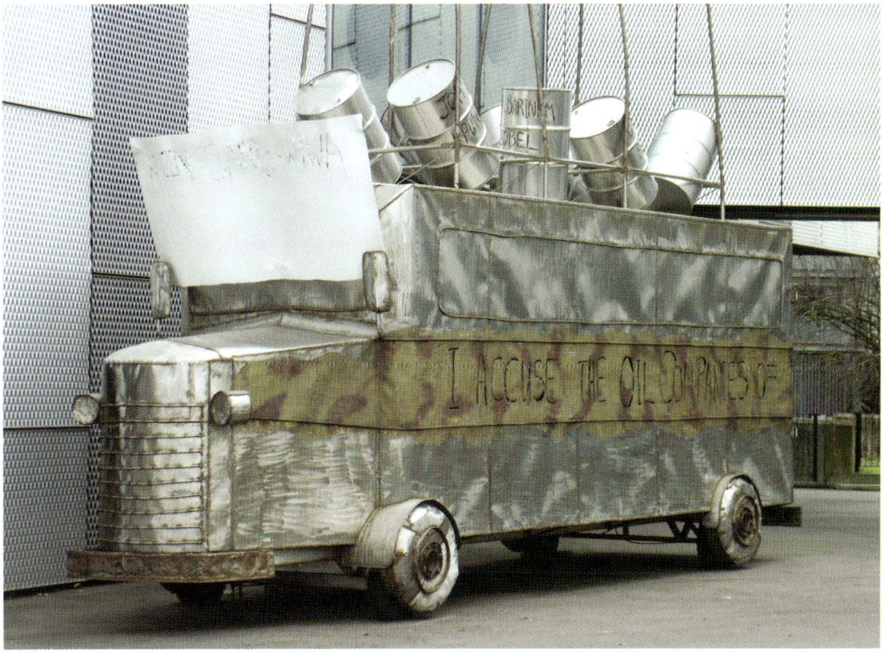

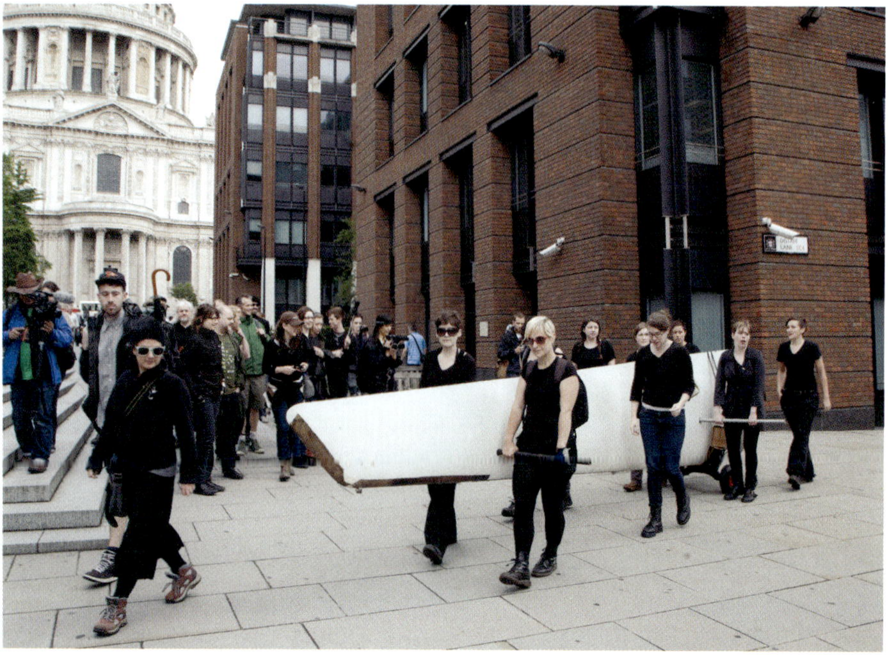

The Gift: In the summer of 2012, Liberate Tate gave a gift to the Tate Modern in protest of the oil company BP and its sponsorship of the Tate's programming. Over 100 members of this coalition of artists and environmental activists collectively recovered an unused wind turbine blade

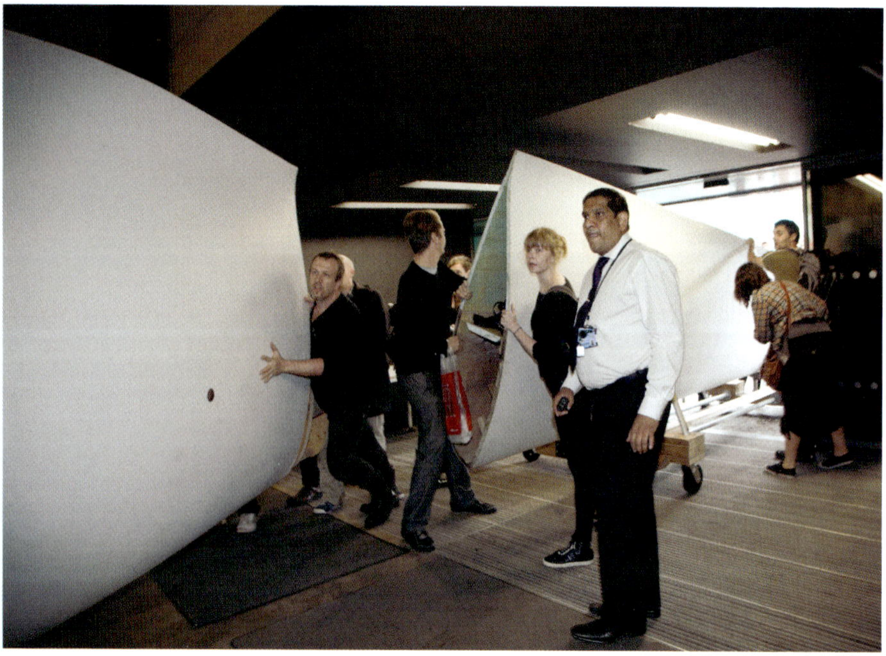

from a valley in Wales, transported it across London, and pushed in through the doors at the Tate Modern to install it as an art work in the Turbine Hall. Liberate Tate also gave the museum documentation that designated the blade as an official "gift to the nation," which requires the museum to officially process the work and consider it for the permanent collection. From Liberate Tate's public communiqué: "Resting on the floor of your museum, it might resemble the bones of a leviathan monster washed up from the salty depths, a suitable metaphor for the deep arctic drilling that BP is profiting from now that the ice is melting. But it is not an animal, nor is it dead, it is a living relic from a future that is aching to become the present. It is part of a magic machine, a tool of transformation, a grateful giant." Photos by Martin LeSanto-Smith, 2012.

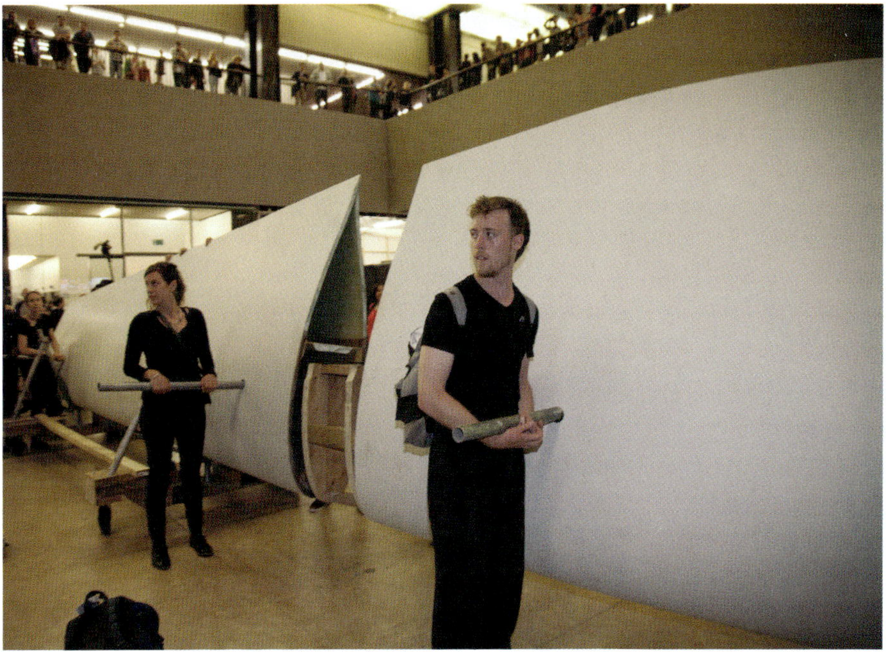

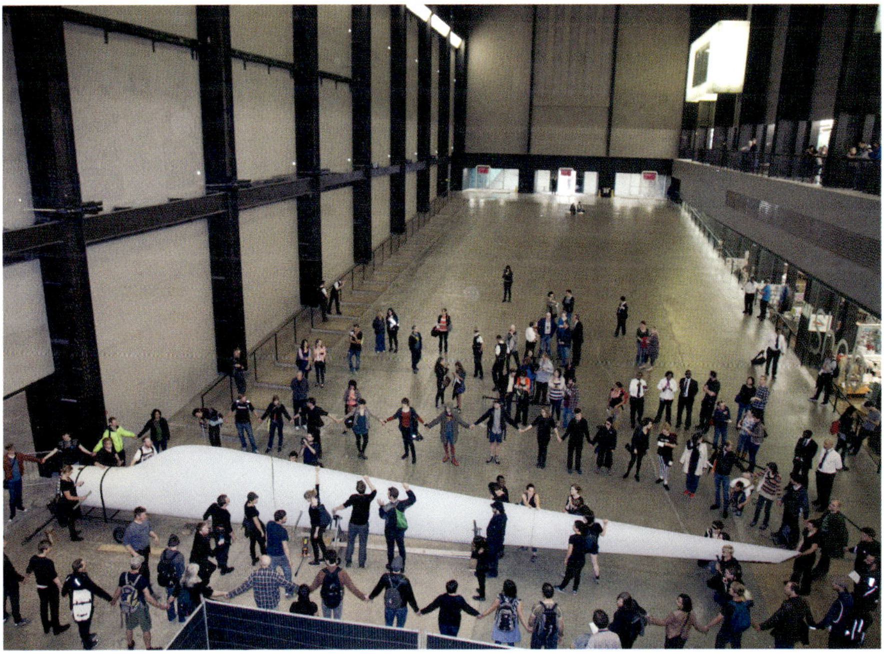

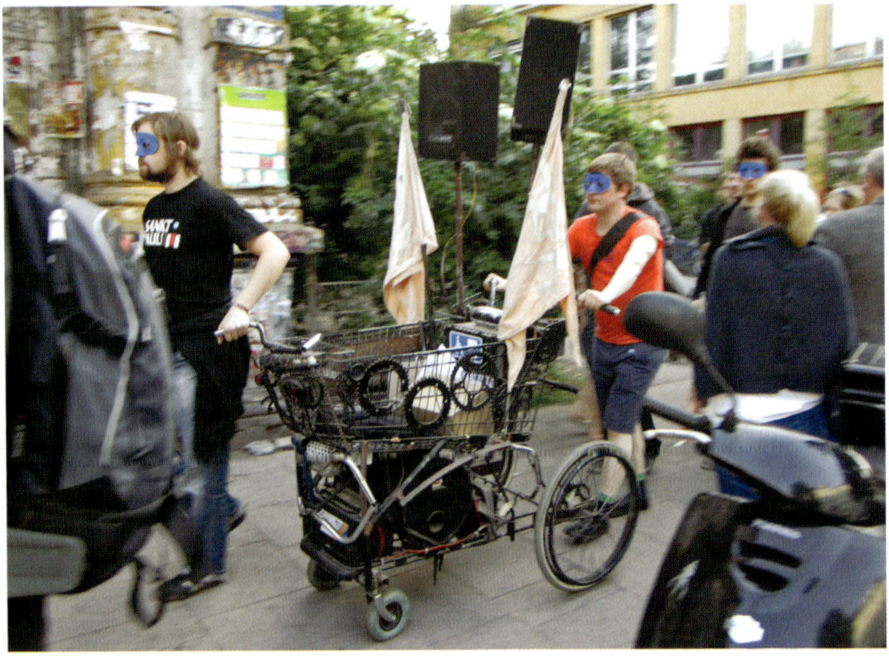

Mobile Sound System: Anti-gentrification-sound-art-qua-booming-techno is best played really damn loud on your own mobile shopping cart sound system. The Hedonist Internationale know how to do it with this set up in Hamburg during the Right to the City Congress, 2011.

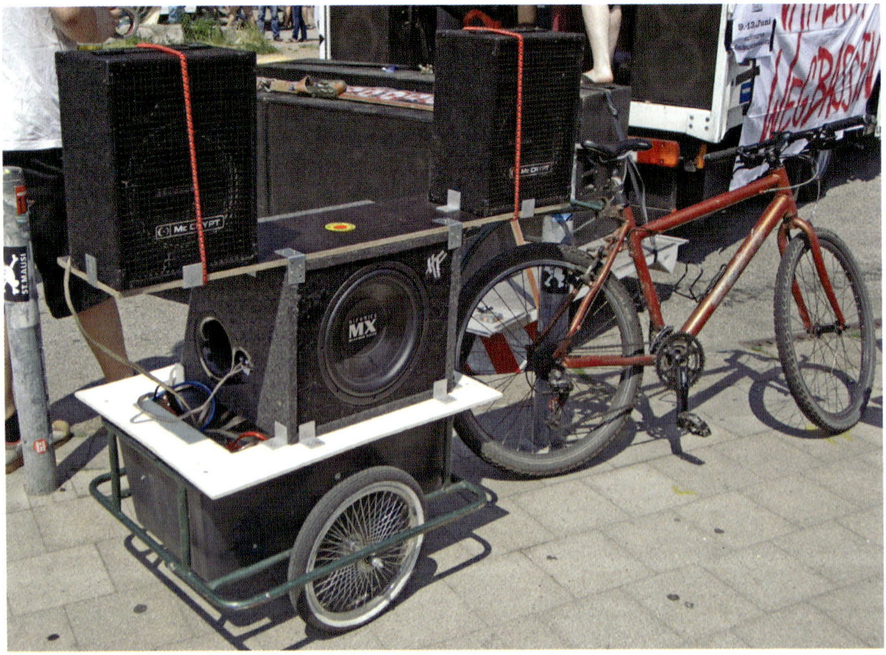

Bike Cart Beats: This sound system was built into a bike cart to be used during protests. There were several innovative mobile sound sytems like this one (and that pictured above) used in Hamburg during The Right to the City Congress, 2011.

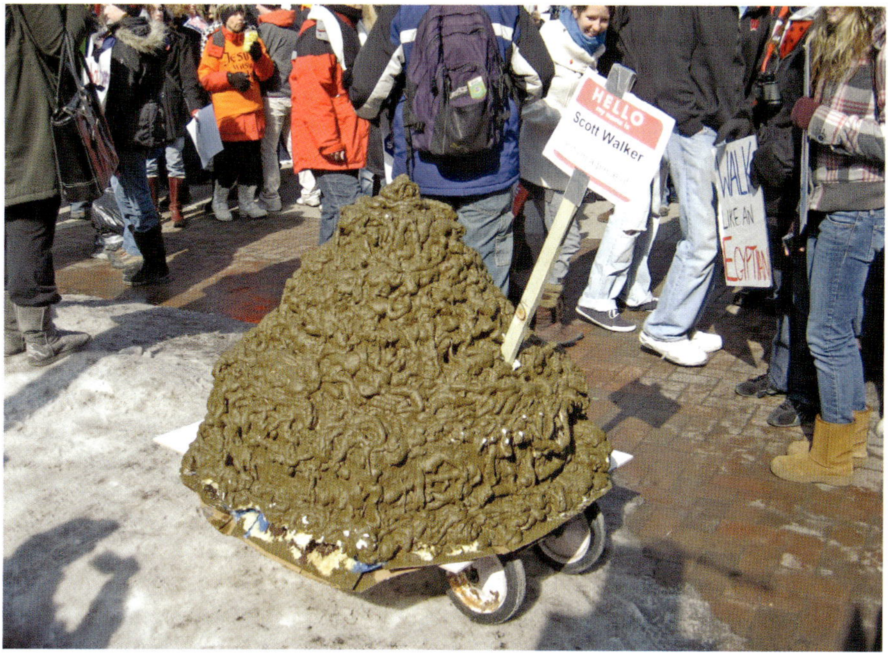

Turd On The Run: A mobile pile of shit claiming to be Wisconsin Governor, Republican Scott Walker. Taken in Madison, Wisconsin at a March 12, 2011, demonstration against Walker's bill stripping unionized state and local government workers of most collective bargaining rights.

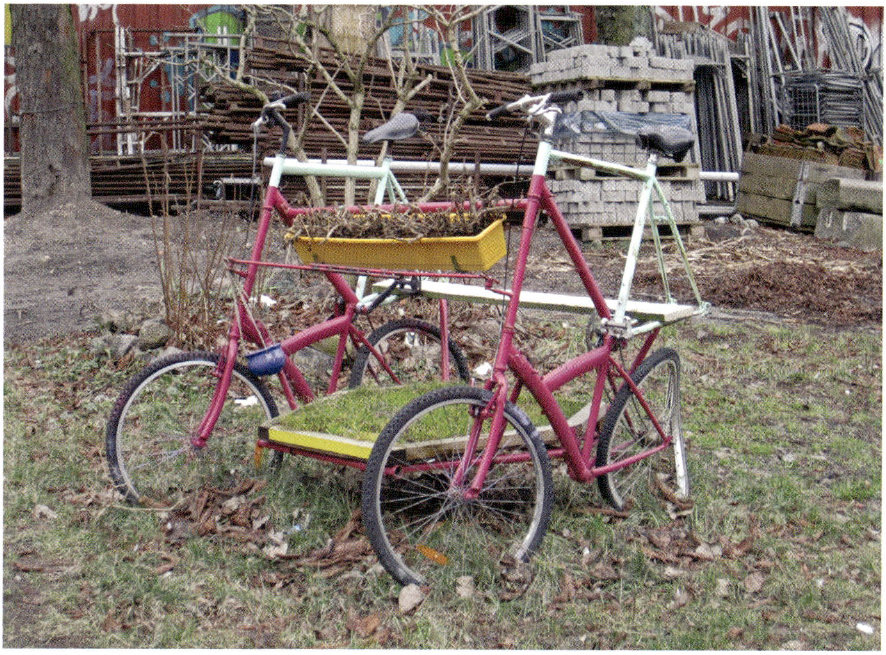

Double Trouble: The remains of an army of bikes by the Bike Bloc & The Laboratory of Insurrectionary Imagination/Climate Camp. Passengers used the frames as a ladder to climb over police barricades during the COP15 climate summit in Copenhagen, Denmark, 2011.

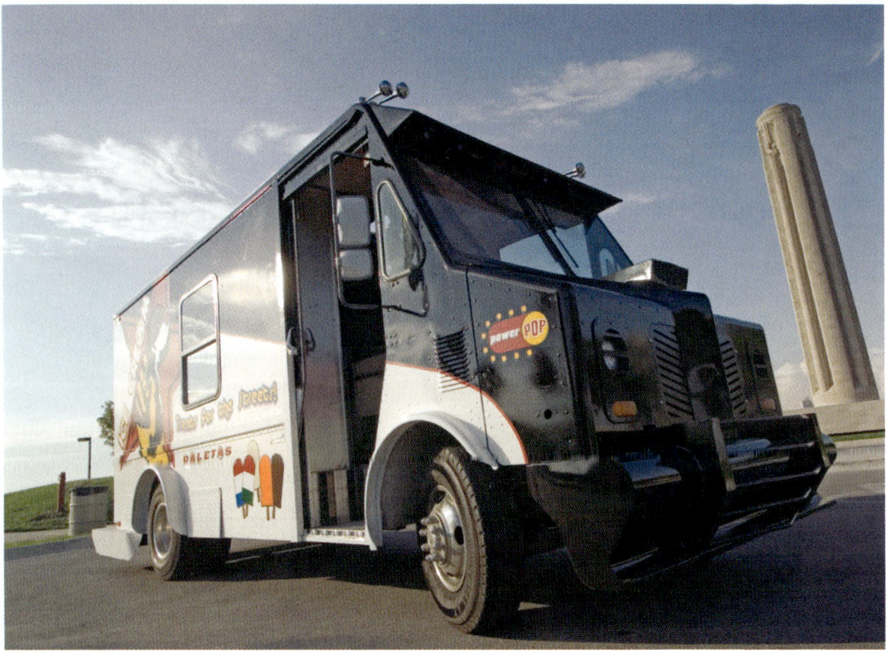

***Tactical Ice Cream Unit* (TICU):** Combining a number of creative activist strategies (Food-Not-Bombs, Copwatch, Indymedia, infoshops, etc.) into one mega-mobile, the TICU is the alter-ego of the cops' mobile command center. The TICU was made by The Center For Tactical

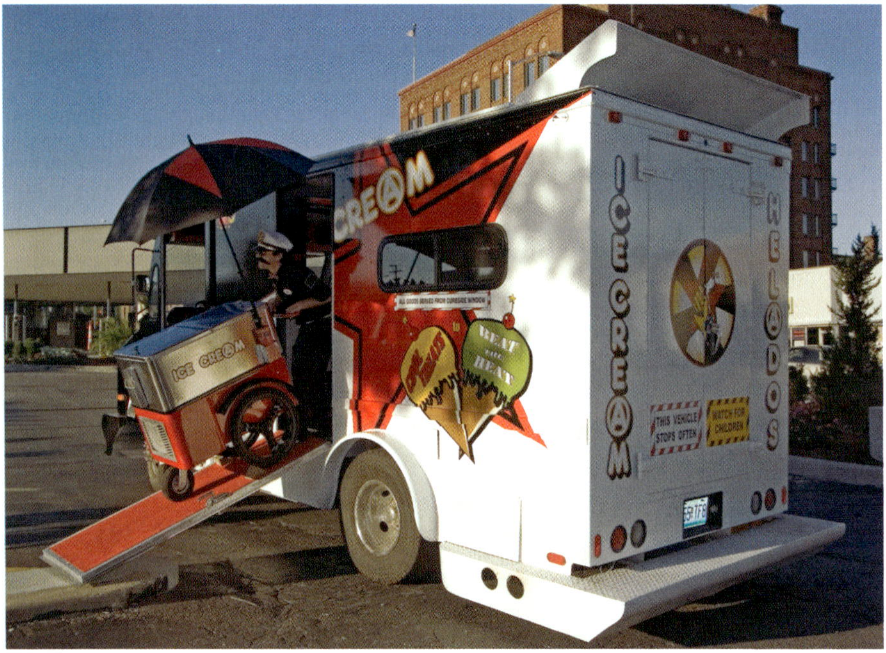

Magic (CTM). Although it appears to be a mild-mannered vending vehicle, it harbors a host of surveillance devices, a booming sound-system, rooftop stage, activist supplies, free wi-fi, and of course, ice cream. With every free ice cream, the sweet-toothed citizenry also receives

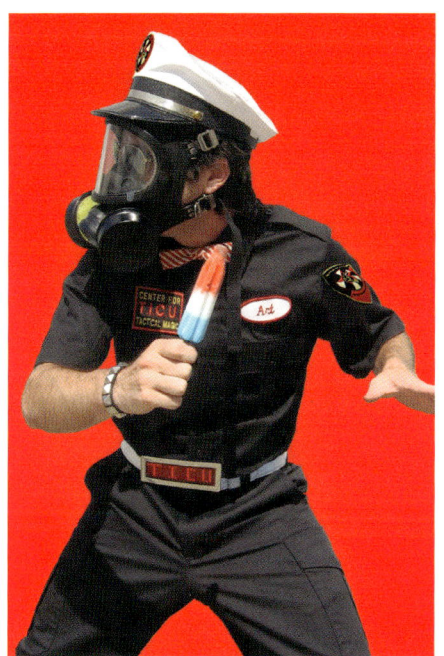 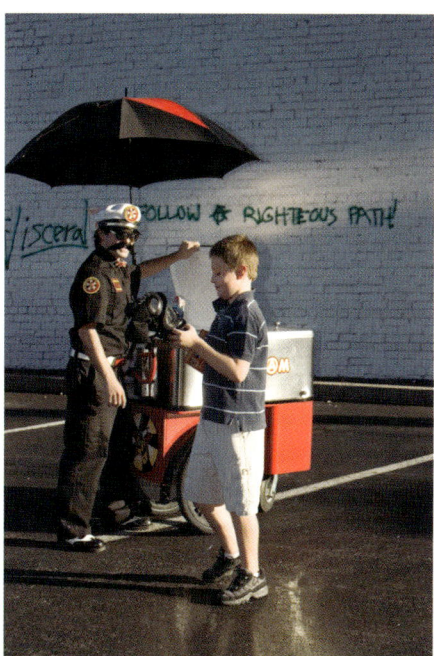

righteous propaganda developed by community groups. Other potential "Pop Ops" include monitoring police activity, running sting operations against corporate dumping, and supporting strikes, rallies, or civil uprisings. Serving as a vehicle both literally and metaphorically, the

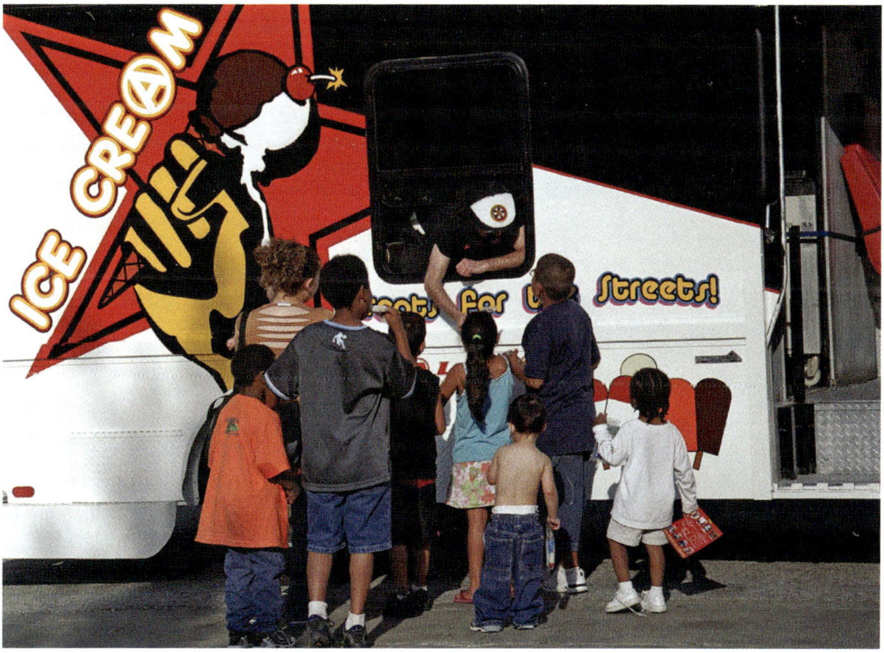

TICU merges activism, car culture, new media performance art, and Homeland Security while providing food-for-thought, good humor, and cool treats to beat the heat. www.tacticalmagic.org. Photos by CTM, 2005-present.

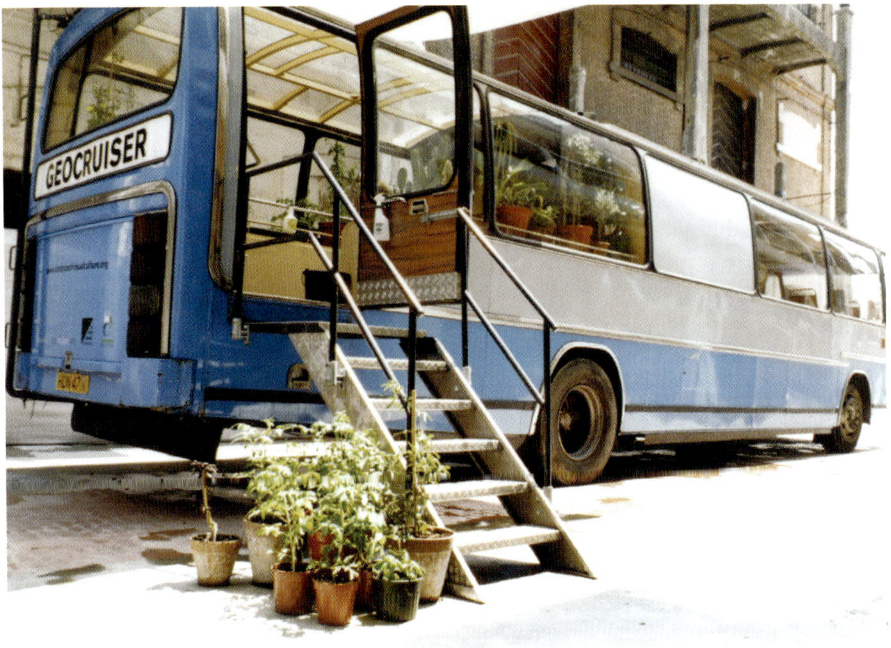

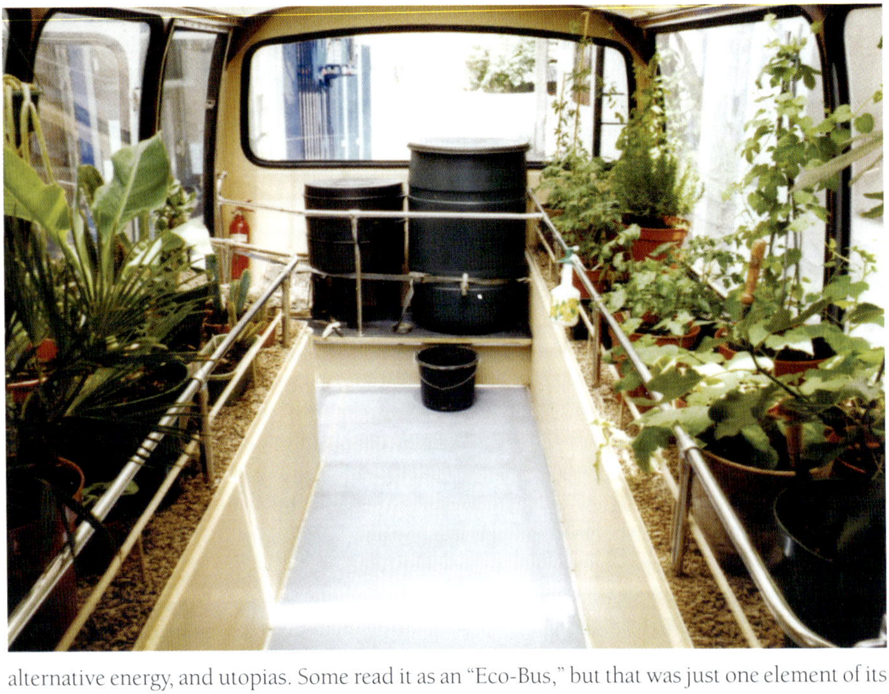

The Geocruiser: In 2001, artist Nils Norman redesigned a coach to have a greenhouse built into the back and a reading room in the front. It contained a small library and information center devoted to gentrification, experimental city design, radical gardening, sustainable design, alternative energy, and utopias. Some read it as an "Eco-Bus," but that was just one element of its function as a mobile propaganda machine. Onboard was a solar-powered photocopier and laptop. It also had its own wormery, used to compost and recycle organic waste. The mobile green-

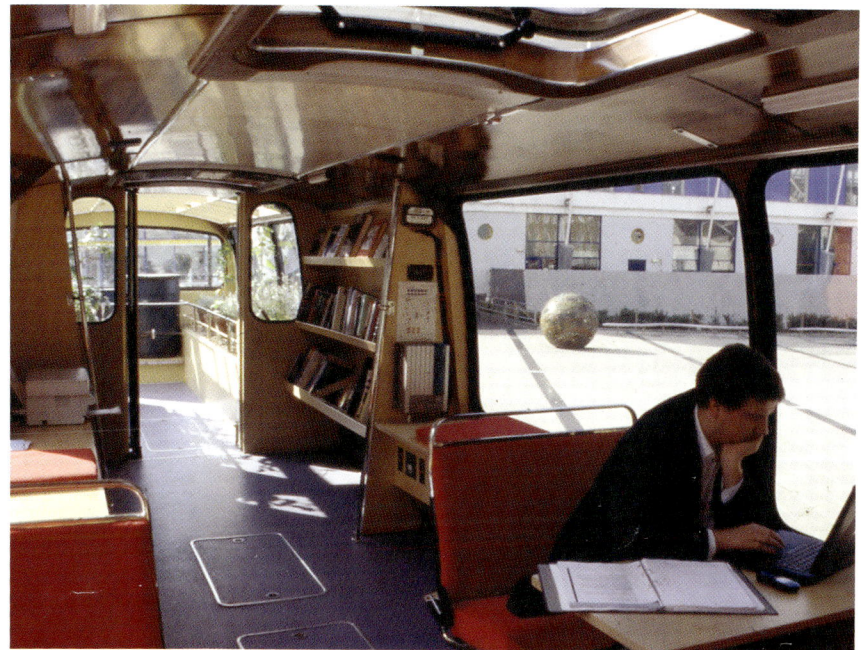

house grew herbs, vegetables, cacti, and succulents. Heavy condensation would form on the inside of the greenhouse's plastic roof panels at night, which would irrigate the plants below as the bus vibrated when started up in the morning. After touring Europe, stopping

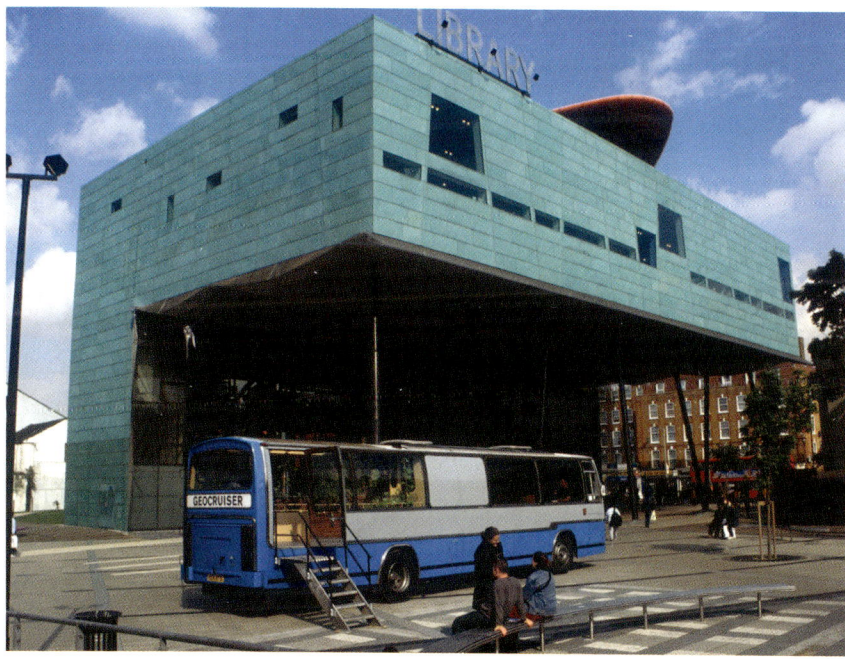

at schools, parks, town squares, museums, and libraries, the *Geocruiser* was decommissioned in 2004. The vehicle was then bought by a family for a nominal fee. They redesigned parts of the interior to make it more livable. Photos by Nils Norman, 2001-2004.

MOBILITY RESOURCES:

Here is a guide to additional information we think is useful to the reader for expanding upon the material covered in the book.

BOOKS:

Acting in Public, Maier, Julia and Rick, Matthias, eds. Berlin: Raumlaborberlin, 2008. Raum Labor is a platform, based in Berlin, interested in making cities more open to experimental temporary uses. The group's *Spacebuster* is a truck from the back of which a large inflatable structure emerges and accommodates up to 80 people. It can easily be moved around for various events and gatherings. This book is filled with ideas for transforming "underestimated" urban spaces in inspiring ways.

Archigram, Cooke, Peter, ed. New York: Princeton Architectural Press, 1999. Among the fascinating projects of this British architecture group are plans for a Walking City.

The Art Trucks of Japan, Kato, Tomoyuki. Tokyo: DH Publishing, 2008. Vibrant color photographs of "dekotora" or "decorated trucks".

Bikes of Burden, Kemp, Hans. Hong Kong: Visionary World Ltd., 2003. Photos by Hans Kemp that document extraordinary uses of motorbikes on the streets of Vietnam.

Bookmobiles and Bookmobile Service, Brown, Eleanor Frances. Metuchen, NJ: The Scarecrow Press, Inc., 1967. Images of everything from Civil War era mobile libraries pulled by horses to libraries in Germany in the 1930s with walls that expand with the flip of switch.

Dwelling Portably: 1980-89, 1990-1999, 2000-2008, Davis, Bert and Holly. Bloomington, IN: Microcosm Publishing, 2008 and 2009. Three separate volumes filled with insights on nomadic living.

Mongo: Adventures in Trash, Botha, Ted. New York: Bloomsbury USA, 2005. Botha tells the stories of New Yorkers who roam the streets seeking any kind of trash that retains value, from edible discards to sellable recyclables and cultural treasures.

Narrative of the Life of Henry Box Brown, Brown, Henry "Box", with